let's talk science

Adventures on Planet Earth

level 3

MASTERBOOKS®
— CURRICULUM —

MASTER BOOKS
— CURRICULUM —

Author: Carrie Lindquist

Master Books Creative Team:

Editor: Willow Meek

Cover and Interior Design:
Diana Bogardus
Terry White

Copy Editors:
Judy Lewis
Willow Meek

Curriculum Review:
Laura Welch
Kristen Pratt
Diana Bogardus

First printing: April 2021

Master Books®, P.O. Box 726, Green Forest, AR 72638
Master Books® is a division of the New Leaf Publishing Group, Inc.

ISBN: 978-1-68344-266-0
ISBN: 978-1-61458-777-4 (digital)

All Scripture quotations, unless otherwise indicated, are taken from the Holy Bible, New International Version®, NIV®. Copyright ©1973, 1978, 1984, 2011 by Biblica, Inc.™ Used by permission of Zondervan. All rights reserved worldwide. www.zondervan.com The "NIV" and "New International Version" are trademarks registered in the United States Patent and Trademark Office by Biblica, Inc.™

Scripture quotations marked (NIrV) are taken from the Holy Bible, New International Reader's Version®, NIrV® Copyright © 1995, 1996, 1998, 2014 by Biblica, Inc.™ Used by permission of Zondervan. All rights reserved worldwide. www.zondervan.com The "NIrV" and "New International Reader's Version" are trademarks registered in the United States Patent and Trademark Office by Biblica, Inc.™

All images are from shutterstock.com, getty.com, or public domain (PD-US), (CC BY-SA 3.0), and Tender Heart Wildlife Rescue.

Printed in the United States of America.

Please visit our website for other great titles: www.masterbooks.com

About the Author

Carrie Lindquist is a homeschool graduate, wife to Wayne, and momma to two energetic boys. She is a passionate advocate for homeschooling and loves helping new-to-homeschooling moms realize that homeschooling through the early years isn't scary — it's really just an extension of all the fun things they are already doing with their children! When she isn't cleaning the endless little messes her boys create, you can find her encouraging moms to embrace the calling of everyday faithfulness.

Introduction to Ecology

Day 1

Oh good! We are so glad you're here! My name is Hannah, and this is my brother Ben. We've been waiting for you to start our science adventure this year! During the summer, we started to explore the places where plants and animals live. We also learned a little about the relationships God created between living and non-living things. It's a type of science called **ecology** (said this way: ĭh-cȧll-ō-jē).

As we explored ecology, though, we found that some people believe all the amazing relationships we see in creation just happened through lots of time and chance. We've learned from the Bible in the Book of Genesis, though, that God created the heavens and the earth. He is the One who designed all the relationships we see in creation.

That's right! God should receive the glory and praise for His design. So now, we're on a mission to find and share God's amazing designs.

In Revelation 4:11, it says:

You are worthy, our LORD and God, to receive glory and honor and power, for you created all things, and by your will they were created and have their being.

As we begin our science adventure, we can pray and ask God to give us insight and wisdom as we explore His creation.

Proverbs 2:3–5 says:

Indeed, if you call out for insight and cry aloud for understanding, and if you look for it as for silver and search for it as for hidden treasure, then you will understand the fear of the LORD and find the knowledge of God.

As we look for and document God's design in creation — like a hidden treasure — we'll also learn more about God. Oh, one more thing — that verse talks about the "fear of the LORD" — that doesn't mean that we'll become scared of God, but that we are amazed by Him and that we respect and follow Him.

So, will you join us on our mission to find and document God's amazing design in His creation? **Let's get started!**

applyit

Prayer is the way we talk to God. As we begin our school adventure each day, we can pray and ask God for insight, wisdom, and understanding as we learn more about Him and the world He made.

Read Genesis 1 and 2 as a family.

DIGGING DEEPER

Day

Before we get started, there are a few words we'll need to learn. My brother Ben is good at keeping track of words and their meanings. Where should we start, Ben?

Let's start with environment! An **environment** (said this way: ĕn-vī-rŭn-mĕnt) is the place a person, plant, or animal lives. The environment includes what the land looks like, what plants grow there, what animals live there, and even the weather patterns.

We talked about ecology in our last lesson — **ecology** is the study of the environment plants and animals live in. Ecology also studies the relationships between living and non-living things.

Perfect! Thanks, Ben! We're going to be building on those words this year as we explore ecology, and I don't want us to lose track of all the words we're going to learn.

Good point, Hannah, I think we need a glossary. A **glossary** (said this way: glŏss-ŭh-rē) is a tool that lists words and their meanings. It's usually found in the back of a book and the words are listed in alphabetical order.

Alphabetical order means that the words that start with the letter A will be listed first. Words that start with the letter B will be next, and so on. If we forget the meaning of a word that was shown in **green**, we can look it up in the glossary.

Let's try it now! Can you find the word **ecology** in the glossary in the back of this book? You can ask your teacher for help if you need to! Once you've found the word, let's go explore our own environment.

applyit Go outside and explore your environment. What types of plants or animals do you see around you? Can you spot two of the same kind of trees or plants? What is the weather like? Is the land around you flat or are there hills and mountains? What do you enjoy about your environment?

Now, draw a picture of your environment. You can show what the land looks like, what plants grow there, what animals live there, and even what the weather is like today.

Day

Have you ever looked at a cake with different layers? Maybe it had a layer of vanilla cake, then a layer of chocolate, then another layer of vanilla, and finally a layer of yummy frosting on top. Ecology is a type of science that has many layers too. As we learn new words, they build on each other like a layered cake or a block tower. Let's learn a few new words today so that we're ready to explore deeper!

We can start with the word habitat. A **habitat** (said this way: hăb-ĭ-tăt) is the natural environment a plant or animal lives in. For example, if you saw a squirrel in the forest, the forest would be the squirrel's habitat.

Ecosystem is also an important word. An **ecosystem** (said this way: ē-cō-sĭs-tŭm) is all of the living and non-living things that are together in a place. Let me think of

an example of an ecosystem — a pond! The water, plants, fish, birds, and animals in and around the pond form an ecosystem.

We have one more word to build on top of that! A **biome** (said this way: bī-ōm) is a very large habitat that contains many of the same types of plants and animals. A biome can be home to many ecosystems, like a pond and a forest.

applyit Let's practice. Can you match each word with the correct meaning?

Habitat

All of the living and non-living things that are together in a place.

Ecosystem

A natural environment that a plant or animal lives in.

Biome

A very large habitat that contains many of the same types of plants and animals.

Day

The earth has several types of biomes. We're going to explore four biomes together this year:

1. the boreal (said this way: bō-rē-ŭhl) forest

2. the deciduous (said this way: dĭh-sĭj-ū-ŭs) forest

3. the grassland

4. the tropical rainforest

We're going to start with the boreal forest. This biome can also be called the taiga (said this way: tī-gŭh). I can't wait to dig into our exploration of the boreal forest!

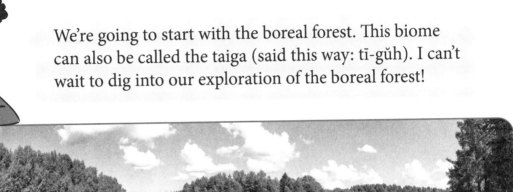

Ecology is all about relationships in creation. One thing that I love about science is how it also teaches me more about God and my relationship with Him. This week, all the talk about habitats, the places we live and dwell, can remind us of Psalm 91:1–2:

Whoever dwells in the shelter of the Most High will rest in the shadow of the Almighty. I will say of the LORD, "He is my refuge and my fortress, my God, in whom I trust."

Sometimes, we get distracted by life and forget to keep our minds and hearts focused on God — to be dwelling in Him as the Psalm talks about. When we get distracted, we also forget that we can trust God — that He is good — and we become fearful and anxious. Have you ever felt fearful and anxious? What is one way you can begin to trust God, to dwell in Him?

When science teaches us more about our relationship with God, it's like finding a hidden treasure that we can share with others!

applyit A biome is a natural habitat that covers a very large amount of land. Biomes can look very different from one another. Let's copy the name of each of the biomes we're going to explore this year!

Boreal Forest

_____
_____
_____
_____

Grassland

_____
_____
_____

Deciduous Forest

_____
_____
_____
_____

Tropical Rainforest

_____
_____
_____
_____

 Memorize all, or part, of Psalm 91:1–2.

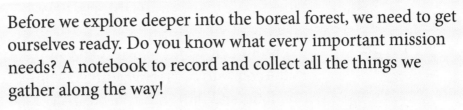

Before we explore deeper into the boreal forest, we need to get ourselves ready. Do you know what every important mission needs? A notebook to record and collect all the things we gather along the way!

Scientists often draw or take a picture of what they observe so that they can share it with others. As we explore God's creation through ecology this year, we're going to compile a Science Notebook. We'll record the things we learn about and the designs God created in our Notebook. Each week you can share what you've learned with someone else, just like a real scientist.

This week we built our vocabulary — **vocabulary** (said this way: vō-căb-ū-lĕh-rē) is a fancy word that means all the words that we know. We talked about our environment, habitats, and biomes. Do you remember what a habitat is? A habitat is the natural environment a plant or animal lives in. Let's add that word to our Science Notebook!

We talked about a squirrel's habitat in the forest, so let's draw a picture of a squirrel. Here's a picture of a squirrel we can look at and the basic shape we can use to draw in our Notebook. You can also use any other picture of a squirrel if you'd like!

Ben and I already added this page to our Notebooks. Ben's squirrel is gathering acorns into a pile in his home. Our little brother Sam even drew a squirrel. His is smiling!

I love how each of our pictures is different; it reminds me of God's creativity. We see God's creativity in creation, in the many different kinds of plants and animals He made. God gave us the ability to be creative just like Him. Each of our pictures is unique, and they show the creativity God has given us.

In your Science Notebook, write: **A habitat is the natural environment a plant or animal lives in.**

Then draw a picture of a squirrel in its habitat.

Learning about habitats this week also reminded us that God is our dwelling place and that we can trust Him. Copy Psalm 91:2 on the back of your Notebook page as a reminder.

I will say of the LORD, "He is my refuge and my fortress, my God, in whom I trust" (*Psalm 91:2*).

The Boreal Forest Climate

Day 1

Are you ready to explore the boreal forest with us? I'm excited to begin, and don't forget about our mission! Remember to look for God's design in this amazing biome. Ben has been reading about the boreal forest to help us get started.

I sure have, and I have some cool things to share with you! The word boreal is a word that means northern regions — and that is right where you'll find the boreal forest biome. Boreal forests are found high in the northern hemisphere (said this way: hĕm-ĭs-fēēr) of the earth.

Wait, can you explain what the northern hemisphere is?

Oh, right! If we were to look at a map or globe of the earth and draw a pretend line around the middle of the earth, the top half would be what we call the northern hemisphere.

At the very top of the northern hemisphere we would find the arctic, or tundra, biome. The arctic might make you think of the penguins, polar bears, ice, and snow that belong there! The arctic is another type of biome that is very cold — so cold, in fact, that no trees grow there, and it's covered in ice and snow most of the year. The boreal forest biome is under the arctic region on a map, and the winters here can be similar to the harsh and bitter cold winters of the arctic region.

dirt	✓
clear bowl or jar	☐
plastic wrap	☐
paper towels	☐
a glass of water	☐

> **Weekly materials list**

The biggest land biome on earth is the boreal forest. Let's look at how much of the earth this biome covers. Write **Boreal Forest Biome** on the line to label the map.

 Most of the world's boreal forest can be found in the country of Russia. In fact, the world's largest boreal forest covers Russia from the Pacific Ocean all the way to the Ural Mountains. Canada is also home to a large boreal biome. Can you find Russia and Canada on this map?

As we begin our exploration of the boreal forest, I think it would be helpful to know more about the weather that plants and animals experience in this environment. Ben, what is another name for the normal weather patterns in an area?

That would be the **climate** (said this way: klī-mĕt). The climate is the usual, or typical, amount of rain, snow, cloud cover, and sunlight an environment (or biome) will experience during a year. Another way to say that is that climate is the normal weather an environment will experience during a year.

For example, the climate in a hot, dry desert will be very different from the climate in a hot and wet rainforest.

The climate in the boreal forest can be extreme and harsh. The winters here can last for 6 months, which is half of the year. Winter days are short and snowy, with little sunlight. The temperatures can reach far, far below 32° Fahrenheit, which is the temperature water freezes at. Plants, people, and animals that live in this environment must be strong to survive. Let's review our new word for today!

applyit Copy this sentence on the lines below: **The climate is the typical weather an environment will experience during a year.**

 Ask your teacher to help you look up the average winter temperatures where you live. What is your **climate** like during the winter?

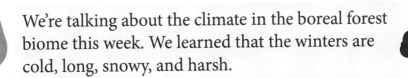

We're talking about the climate in the boreal forest biome this week. We learned that the winters are cold, long, snowy, and harsh.

What are summers like in the boreal forest?

Good question! Summers are short, but they can be warm — even hot — and humid. We also find a lot of swamps and bogs in the boreal forest. These are areas where the rain causes some land to stay wet and soggy. The boreal forest is a land of extremes with cold, harsh winters and hot, humid summers.

I wonder why the land stays wet and soggy in some areas of the boreal forest?

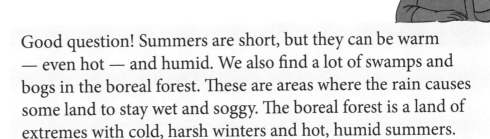

In most biomes, water from rain will drain through the soil and flow underground. We call it groundwater. Groundwater may be used by plants, and it can also flow underground to a stream, lake, or ocean.

In the boreal biome, though, water can't always drain through the soil. Underneath the soil here there is often bedrock. Bedrock is a long, hard layer of rock. There can also be permafrost.

Oh! I read about permafrost last night! **Permafrost** is a layer of ground that stays hard and frozen all year long. Permafrost can start just a few inches deep under your feet, or it can be far below the surface. The long, cold winter causes the ground to freeze, but the summer isn't hot or long enough to thaw it all the way. So, permafrost stays frozen all the time.

Permafrost creates a solid layer of earth. Water from melting ice and snow, as well as rain, cannot drain through it. Permafrost keeps water near the surface of the boreal biome, and it helps the plants and animals that live there. Would you like to see how permafrost works?

Activity directions:

1. Stretch 2–3 paper towels over the top of the bowl or jar — you may need someone to help you hold it in place.

2. Place some of the dirt on top of the paper towel.

3. Now, slowly pour some of the water over the dirt. What happens? The water will sink through the dirt and some of the water will be absorbed by the paper towel. The rest of the water drains through to the bowl.

4. Now, remove the paper towel and empty the bowl.

5. Stretch the plastic wrap over the top of the bowl and add dirt to the top.

6. Slowly pour water over the dirt again, what happens this time? The water cannot drain through the plastic wrap, so it stays around the dirt in a puddle. The plastic wrap acts like permafrost and keeps the water trapped above.

7. Be sure to clean up after your activity!

Permafrost and bedrock are important parts of the boreal biome. They help keep water from draining away through the soil. In the harshest areas of the boreal forest, water can be hard to find, but bedrock and permafrost help to keep it available for the plants and animals.

If it wasn't for permafrost and bedrock keeping water trapped near the surface, the plants wouldn't have water and they couldn't survive. If the plants can't survive, the birds and animals would have nothing to eat either! This is just one important relationship in the boreal forest. We're going to learn about so many more!

Sometimes, all that water trapped sitting on the surface creates a swamp or bog and it can be, well, awful stinky! I was thinking about stinky swamps today, and it reminded me of un-forgiveness. Have you ever been angry or hurt by something someone did or said? I know I have!

If we stay angry and do not forgive someone else, it slowly begins to make our hearts bitter and hard. All that anger pools up inside of our hearts, just like water over permafrost or bedrock, and it makes our attitudes and actions nasty and stinky. Unforgiveness can make a stinky, swampy mess inside of our hearts!

Colossians 3:12–13 tells us:

You are God's chosen people. You are holy and dearly loved. So put on tender mercy and kindness as if they were your clothes. Don't be proud. Be gentle and patient. Put up with one another. Forgive one another if you are holding something against someone. Forgive, just as the Lord forgave you (NIRV).

We can show mercy, kindness, and forgiveness to others because we know that God has also forgiven us. When we forgive, we follow His example. What a neat lesson from permafrost!

Talk about forgiveness as a family. Have you or someone else in your family forgiven someone, even if it was hard?

It's time to add a page to our Science Notebook today! We've explored the boreal climate a little, and we also explored permafrost. Permafrost helps keep water available in the boreal biome, and I see God's wisdom in that.

Let's add permafrost to our Notebook this week! Here is a picture we can look at to give us an idea for our drawing.

We'll let you see our drawings too. Hannah and I used colored pencils. Sam used markers to give his brighter colors. We all even added a little bit of glitter glue to make our permafrost sparkle. Have fun using the creativity God has given you as you add permafrost to your Notebook!

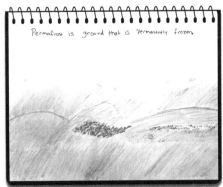

In your Science Notebook, write: **Permafrost is ground that is permanently frozen.**

Then draw a picture showing permafrost — and don't forget to show someone else and tell them all about what you learned this week!

 Learning about permafrost and swamps this week reminded us that un-forgiveness can create a stinky mess inside our hearts too. Copy Colossians 3:13 on the back of your Notebook page as a reminder that the Lord forgave us and we can forgive others too.

Put up with one another. Forgive one another if you are holding something against someone. Forgive, just as the Lord forgave you (Colossians 3:13; NIrV).

Conifers

Day 1

Hi, friend! Ben and I are ready to explore deeper into the boreal forest with you this week. The boreal biome covers a lot of the northern hemisphere, but we're going to explore one certain place: Yellowstone National Park.

Yellowstone National Park covers almost 3,400 square miles in the United States. It's huge! Most of Yellowstone is located in the state of Wyoming, but some of the park is also located in Idaho and Montana. Yellowstone National Park is part of the boreal biome — but because it is so big, it also stretches into other biomes.

We visited Yellowstone National Park last year on our family vacation, and we learned a lot! Ben, do you remember what the climate was like at Yellowstone?

Oh yes! As part of the boreal biome, the weather can be harsh and change really fast. Winters are long and cold, and the temperature can fall way below freezing. Over 12 feet of snow can fall in some parts of the park during the year. That's a lot of snow! In the summer, the temperature is often around 70° Fahrenheit and there can be lots of thunderstorms.

Interesting! It sounds like plants and animals that live in Yellowstone National Park need to be tough to survive. I think we're going to spot God's design here! I'm looking forward to exploring deeper; for now, though, let's find Wyoming, Idaho, and Montana on a map!

- 2 pieces of construction paper ✓
- Scissors
- Tape
- Flour
- Baking sheet or plate

Weekly materials list

applyit Circle Wyoming, Idaho, and Montana on the United States map.

Day

Today, let's explore the types of trees that grow at Yellowstone National Park! Conifer trees are the most common trees and they —

Whoa, whoa, whoa Ben! What is a conifer tree?

Oh, right, we often call them pine trees. **Conifers** (said this way: kå-nĭh-furs) are trees that have needles on their branches instead of leaves. We can also call them coniferous (said this way: kå-nĭh-fur-ŭs) trees.

The needles usually do not turn brown or fall off during the winter — that is why we sometimes call them "evergreen" trees, because most conifer trees stay green throughout the whole year. Conifers usually make pinecones to protect their seeds. There are many types of conifer trees, and you can find nine of them in Yellowstone!

That's neat! Do any other types of trees grow in Yellowstone National Park?

Yes, some deciduous trees also grow there. **Deciduous** (said this way: dĭh-sĭj-ū-ŭs) trees have leaves that fall off the tree before winter. Some leaves turn beautiful shades of red, orange, or yellow in the fall before they fall off the tree. Quaking Aspen is one important type of deciduous tree that grows at Yellowstone. We're going to talk more about that one later on!

Sounds good, Ben. Let's review those new words!

applyit Copy this sentence on the lines below: **Conifers are a type of tree that have needles and usually produce pinecones.**

_____

_____

_____

_____

_____

_____

_____

_____

Copy this sentence on the lines below: **Deciduous trees have leaves that fall off before winter.**

_____

_____

_____

_____

_____

_____

_____

_____

What types of trees grow in your yard or neighborhood? Can you spot any **conifer** or **deciduous** trees?

I studied conifer trees last night and I learned some interesting things about them! Conifer trees are well designed to live in a harsh climate, like the boreal forest. Let's talk about them today — and keep a lookout for ways God designed these trees! We'll first need to start with **photosynthesis** (said this way: fō-tō-sĭn-the-sĭs).

Hannah and I learned about photosynthesis in *Adventures in Creation*. Let's review it quickly! **Photosynthesis** is the process plants use to convert sunlight and carbon dioxide gas from the air into sugar that the plant uses and oxygen that we can breathe.

Leaves and needles have **chlorophyll** (said this way: klōr-ō-fĭll) inside them. Chlorophyll is what causes the leaves and needles to have a green color. The leaves and needles also contain water the tree has drawn up from the soil through its roots.

When the sun shines on the leaves or needles, chlorophyll uses the sunlight to create sugar and oxygen from the water and carbon dioxide inside the leaf. This is the process of photosynthesis! When we talk about the process of photosynthesis, we can use the word **photosynthesize** (said this way: fō-tō-sĭn-the-sīze).

Here is an image that shows how photosynthesis works. Let's write the word **photosynthesis** on the line below!

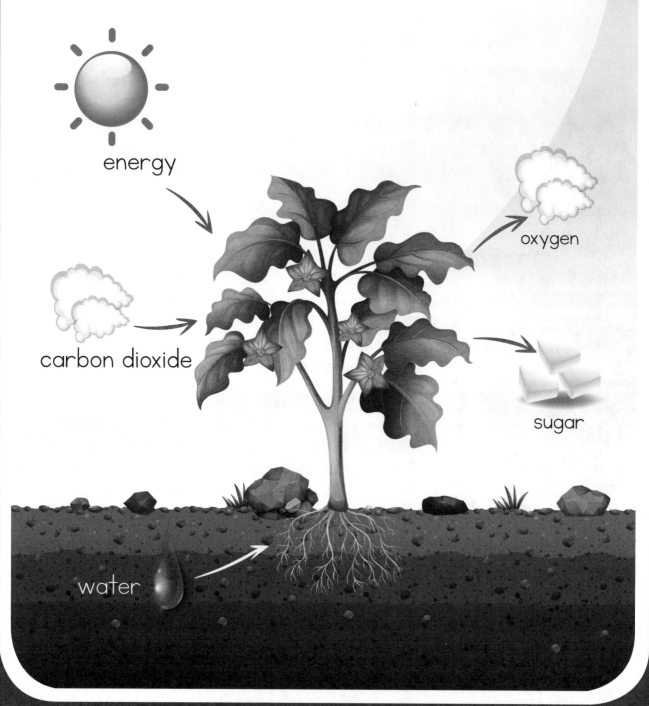

I have a question for you today, Ben! The needles on a conifer tree are much smaller than the broad leaves on a deciduous tree — do you think needles or leaves can photosynthesize better?

Hmm, I would think the leaf, since it is bigger than a needle!

That's what I thought too, but the conifer's needles are actually designed to photosynthesize better than the leaves on a deciduous tree. This is important during the short winter days when there may not be very much sunlight at all, and it's one of the reasons a conifer can keep its needles all year round.

I see God's design and care for creation in that, Hannah!

Me too! The triangle shape of the conifer tree is also important because it allows more needles to receive sunlight. The broad leaves of a deciduous tree often block sunlight for the leaves below it, but the narrow needles and shape of conifer trees allows more needles to receive sunlight at the same time.

The needles also have a thick, waxy coating that helps to protect them and keeps water from evaporating from the tree. This is an important thing during the winter when water is frozen and can be hard to get. That waxy coating also makes the needles slick, which can help snow slide off of the flexible branches. This helps to protect the branches from breaking under a heavy load of snow.

Do you see God's design? He made conifer trees to keep their needles all year, and He gave them a special shape and needle design so that they can grow and thrive even in harsh environments. That is amazing!

materials needed

- [ ] 2 pieces of construction paper
- [ ] Scissors
- [ ] Tape
- [ ] Flour
- [ ] Baking sheet or plate

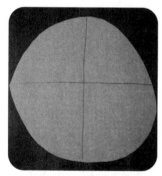

Let's do an activity to see how the triangular shape helps keep too much snow from settling on the branches.

Activity directions:

1. Crumple the first sheet of paper into a ball and place it on the tray. This one will represent the rounded shape and leaves of a deciduous tree.

2. Be sure to ask your teacher for help! Cut a big circle out of the second sheet of paper.

3. Use a pencil to draw a line through the middle of the circle from top to bottom (vertically) and then draw a line through the middle of the circle from left to right (horizontally). You'll make a cross shape on the circle — and it will look a bit like 4 slices of pie on the circle.

4. Now, cut along the lines of one pie slice and remove just that piece.

5. Take the two corners from the slice you cut and fold them in. One will go underneath and one will stay on top, forming a cone. Tape the outside corner to hold your cone together and place the cone on the tray. This one represents a conifer tree with its triangular, cone-like shape and slick needles.

6. Next, pinch some flour between your fingers. We'll pretend the flour is snow. Slowly let it fall onto the crumpled paper. Do the same to the cone. Does more flour gather on the crumpled paper or the cone paper?

The flour gathered on the crumpled piece of paper just like snow does on deciduous trees if the snow comes before they lose their leaves in the fall. This can cause deciduous tree limbs to split and break under the weight of the snow. But a conifer's shape and slick needles help keep too much snow from gathering because the snow can slide off, just like our cone let the flour slide right off.

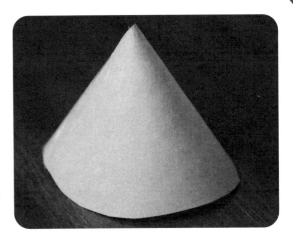

Day

What a week of fun we've had learning about conifers! And now it's my favorite day — the day we add a page to our Science Notebook! We were able to see some of God's design that enables conifers to thrive even when they're not growing in an easy environment.

Our lives aren't always easy either. Sometimes things can feel like a warm, sunny summer day and everything is going well. But other times, life can feel like a cold, hard winter. Conifers were given the design they need to thrive even during the cold, hard winter, and that reminds me of how God also cares for us and helps us through the hardest times.

Psalm 1 talks about a person who follows God's ways, and verse 3 says:

That person is like a tree planted by streams of water, which yields its fruit in season and whose leaf does not wither — whatever they do prospers.

When we follow and trust in the Lord, we can keep growing in Him and blessing others even in the hardest times. When I think of conifers, I'm reminded of Psalm 1:3.

I think they will remind me of Psalm 1:3 from now on too! Let's draw some conifer trees in our Science Notebook today. We can look at this picture for an idea. We can even use some glitter glue to add a little snow to our tree and the ground if we'd like.

In your Science Notebook, write: **God designed conifers to thrive, even during cold winters.**

Then draw a picture of one, or a few, conifers. You can add some glitter glue too if you'd like to add some snow. Don't forget to show someone else and tell them all about God's design in the conifer tree's shape and needles!

Learning about coniferous trees this week also reminded us that life isn't always easy, but God cares for us even during hard times. Copy Psalm 1:3 on the back of your Notebook page as a reminder.

That person is like a tree planted by streams of water, which yields its fruit in season and whose leaf does not wither — whatever they do prospers (Psalm 1:3).

The Lodgepole Pine

Day 1

Last week, we learned a bit about conifer trees. Conifers have needles that usually don't fall off before the winter. We also learned a few ways conifers are designed to thrive even during the winter. Conifer trees photosynthesize well and protect water within the tree.

There are many types of coniferous trees, and nine types grow in Yellowstone. But there's one kind of conifer that makes up most of the forests in the park. Do you remember what tree that is, Ben?

I sure do — the lodgepole pine (said this way: lŏj-pōle pīne). Because these conifers grow tall and straight, Native American tribes near these forests often used lodgepole pine trees to build lodges or tipis. That is how these trees got their name. If you look closely at a lodgepole pine branch, you'll see that the needles grow in groups of two.

Lodgepole pines can create a dense forest with many trees standing close to one another.

Being close together isn't really good for the lodgepole pine trees because they won't have space to grow. It also makes it hard for sunlight to reach all the tree's branches, and lodgepole pines do not like being in the shade. That is why you'll see that lodgepole pines growing together in a forest will often be missing branches on the bottom part of the tree. If the branches near the ground do not receive enough sunlight, they will die and fall off.

As the tree grows taller, the bare, branchless trunk will grow up higher too. Once the tree is fully grown, it may only have branches near the top of the tree.

Interesting! I'm looking forward to learning more about the lodgepole pine this week.

 There are nine types of conifer trees that grow in Yellowstone National Park. Each type of tree is shown below.

lodgepole pine

white spruce

Douglas-fir

whitebark pine

Rocky Mountain juniper

limber pine

common juniper

Engelmann spruce

subalpine fir

Each tree looks slightly different, but what is something they all have?

Day

I wonder why the lodgepole pine can grow so well in Yellowstone National Park?

Let's start with nutrients. **Nutrients** (said this way: new-trēē-ĕnts) are substances that plants, animals, and people need to grow and live. For example, you receive nutrients like vitamins and minerals from the food you eat. Your body uses those nutrients to help you grow and move. If a plant, animal, or person cannot get good nutrients, they may stop growing and become sick.

A tree or plant draws in water and nutrients from the soil through its roots. These nutrients will help the plant or tree grow and live. In the boreal biome, the soil is often acidic, or high in acid.

Yuck! Vinegar is acidic isn't it?

It is! **Acidic** soil is more difficult for plants to grow in because it does not have enough of the nutrients a plant needs.

Well, I'm not surprised! I accidentally took a sip of vinegar this week. I don't think that acidic stuff would help me grow and thrive either!

Oh, Ben, you're so funny! Lodgepole pines actually like to grow in acidic soil. They can survive even when the soil doesn't have the nutrients in it that other trees need.

applyit Copy this sentence on the lines below: **Nutrients** are substances that plants, animals, and people need to grow and live.

Copy this sentence on the lines below: **Acidic** means high in acid.

Sometimes when we study God's creation, we find His mercy — even in our imperfect world. In Genesis we read that God created a perfect world with no sickness, sadness, or death. He also made the first two people, Adam and Eve. God put them in a perfect garden.

God gave Adam and Eve one rule — to not eat the fruit from the tree of the knowledge of good and evil. They chose to disobey God and eat the fruit, and it changed the world. Because of their sin, we no longer live in a perfect creation. We see sickness, sadness, and death around us.

But God is merciful, and we can still see His amazing design even in our imperfect world.

We see one example of God's mercy in forest fires. During thunderstorms, lightning may hit a tree. This can cause a fire that burns through the forest. A forest fire can destroy a lot of the forest. It can be a very sad thing.

Many forest fires have happened in the lodgepole pine forests of Yellowstone. You might think a fire would be the end of the lodgepole pine forest. How could it grow back after being destroyed? Well, pinecones help to protect the tree's seeds, and God designed lodgepole pines to make two types of pinecones.

The first type of pinecone scatters its seed once it is ready. But the other type of pinecone is tightly sealed and protected with resin. This pinecone cannot open up and release the seeds without heat.

Like the heat of a forest fire!

As the fire burns through the forest, it creates the heat that opens up the special sealed pinecones so that new seeds can spread and grow once the fire is over. Those new seeds will begin to grow into a whole new lodgepole pine forest.

In our imperfect world, forest fires are important to the boreal biome. In His wisdom and mercy, God also gave the plants and trees in this environment a way to come back and thrive, even after a forest fire.

applyit   Let's find these words in the word search below:

conifer   pinecone   Yellowstone   resin   fire   mercy

Q	X	C	O	N	I	F	E	R	K	X
M	P	W	C	V	N	I	M	E	J	B
E	F	O	R	Q	P	R	T	S	L	F
R	L	D	J	F	G	E	H	I	B	I
C	K	P	I	N	E	C	O	N	E	R
Y	E	L	L	O	W	S	T	O	N	E

Day

Yesterday we learned about the relationship between forest fires and the special lodgepole pinecones. Isn't it amazing that God designed a special pinecone for the lodgepole pine that can be opened by fire so that new seeds can grow?

I've been wondering, though . . . we learned yesterday that forest fires are also important to the boreal biome. How could that be?

We'll need to start with decomposition. **Decomposition** (said this way: dē-cŏm-pō-zĭ-shŭn) is the process in which dead plants and animals break back down into the soil. For example, if you live in an area with deciduous trees, you'll see the leaves fall off the tree in the fall. But by springtime, you may not be able to find any trace of those leaves because they have decomposed.

In the boreal biome, old, dead plants or tree limbs fall to the forest floor. But there isn't a way for them to decompose very well in this biome. It will take a long time for that material to break back down into the soil.

There are many relationships in other biomes that help material decompose much faster. We'll learn about them later on! But in the boreal biome, all that dead matter on the forest floor begins to build up.

All that material can keep water from getting to the soil and makes it harder for the plants to grow. While it does destroy the old forest, a forest fire helps the boreal forest in many ways. First, it cleans up the forest floor and removes all that old debris (said this way: deh-brie).

After a fire, there will be more water available for the plants that begin to grow again. The trees can grow stronger because they are not crowded anymore. The fire will burn away old and sick trees so that the forest can grow back healthier. The ashes from a fire return nutrients to the soil, which will help a new forest grow well. It also allows sunlight to reach the forest floor, which means grasses and bushes can grow again.

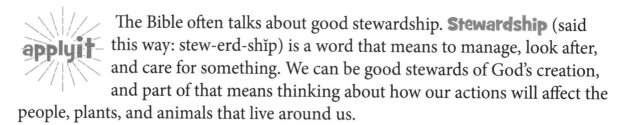

applyit   The Bible often talks about good stewardship. **Stewardship** (said this way: stew-erd-shĭp) is a word that means to manage, look after, and care for something. We can be good stewards of God's creation, and part of that means thinking about how our actions will affect the people, plants, and animals that live around us.

While forest fires can be helpful to the forest, they can also grow out of control and be extremely destructive. Sometimes, forest fires happen naturally from lightning. But other times, people may accidentally cause a forest fire. Ask your teacher to help you research ways you can help prevent forest fires in your area — this is one way you can be a good steward of God's creation! Then, create a picture to show the ways you can prevent forest fires where you live.

I enjoyed learning about the lodgepole pine and forest fires this week. A forest fire is a sad thing, but it also clears the forest of old, dead trees and debris on the forest floor. It helps to clean the boreal environment and creates healthy soil for a brand-new forest to grow. I see God's wisdom and mercy in that!

You know, even though a forest fire can destroy a large area, it also brings something good back to that area — a new, healthy, and strong forest can begin to grow. That reminds me of Joseph's story in the Bible. His brothers betrayed him, people lied and forgot about him, and he was even sent to prison for something he didn't do! Joseph had many sad things happen in his life, but he trusted God and let God continue to grow his faith.

You can read Joseph's story as a family in Genesis chapters 37 and 39–47.

God never left Joseph, and He had a plan for Joseph's life even when he was stuck alone in prison. Later in the story, God used Joseph to save the lives of many, many people — including Joseph's own brothers and family!

In Genesis 50:20, Joseph told his brothers:

You intended to harm me, but God intended it for good to accomplish what is now being done, the saving of many lives.

That can remind us of Romans 8:28 too:

And we know that in all things God works for the good of those who love him, who have been called according to his purpose.

Let's memorize Romans 8:28 together as we draw a picture of the lodgepole pine's special pinecone — and don't forget to tell someone how God can work all things together for the good of those who love Him.

In your Science Notebook, write: **A lodgepole pine tree's pinecone protects the seeds.**

Then, draw a picture of a branch with a pinecone. You can use this one for an idea!

Hidden Treasure

This week, forest fires reminded us that God works all things together for the good of those who love Him. Copy Romans 8:28 on the back of your Notebook page as a reminder.

And we know that in all things God works for the good of those who love him, who have been called according to his purpose (Romans 8:28).

The Food Chain I

Day 1

Hey there, friend! Ready to continue our mission this week? It's time to shift our focus to a different part of ecology now.

Ecology is all about relationships. We're going to explore the connections within creation through the food chain.

Wait, the food chain? Is that like a metal chain that you eat? Because that doesn't sound like a very good snack!

Oh, Ben, you can't eat metal chains! The **food chain** means the links between plants and animals as they eat. Let's say a mouse eats a flower. The flower and the mouse are links in the food chain. After the mouse eats the flower, a snake comes along and eats the mouse. Now, the flower, mouse, and snake are links in the food chain. Later on, a hawk swoops down and eats the snake. Together, the flower, mouse, snake, and hawk create a food chain.

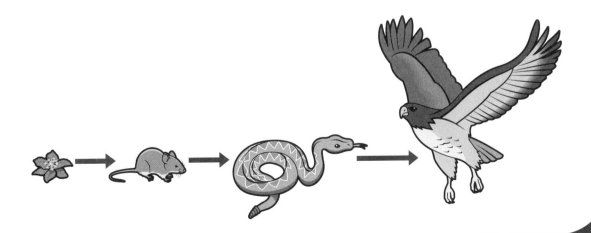

Oh, well, that makes more sense!

applyit

Let's put this food chain back in order. Look at the image of the food chain in our lesson and then label the pictures below from 1 to 4 in the order the chain should go.

There are many types of snakes. You can learn more about rattlesnakes in *God's Big Book of Animals*, available through Master Books®.

Hey, Ben, do you know where the food chain starts?

Hmm, well, with plants, I guess?

Almost — it actually starts with energy (said this way: ĕn-er-jēē). **Energy** allows work to be done. There are many different ways work can be done. For example, plants use energy to photosynthesize, and living things use energy to move around.

In the food chain, plants are called **producers** (said this way prō-doo-sers) because they can produce, or make, their own food through photosynthesis, using energy from the sun.

So the food chain is about energy?

Yes, people and animals get the energy they need to live and work when they eat. The food chain shows how energy moves through creation from the sun, to plants, to animals, to other animals, and even to people.

A plant uses the energy from the sun to create food for itself, sugar. The mouse eats the plant, which gives it energy to move. When the snake eats the mouse, it gets energy as well.

So energy just keeps moving along, it isn't ever used up?

Right — and did you know there are actually laws in science? This is one of the laws, that energy cannot be created or destroyed, but it can change from one form to another form. This is called the first law of thermodynamics (said this way: therm-ō-dī-năm-ĭks).

Well, that is interesting! You know, I've noticed as we've been studying that creation is very organized. It follows patterns, like the seasons, and now we know it follows laws too.

Good point, Ben. I read in 1 Corinthians 14:33 today that God is a God of order and peace. As we learn about the laws God designed creation to follow and we see the organization He placed in creation, it also shows us part of God's character.

applyit

Character is a word that means the qualities of someone. The Bible tells us about the character of God, who He is. Ask your teacher to help you look up these verses in the Bible. What do they teach you about the character of God?

Deuteronomy 7:9

God is

Deuteronomy 32:4

God is

Psalm 147:5

God is

Romans 11:33

God is

1 Corinthians 14:33

God is

I'm ready to get started today! It's fun to learn more about God's creation and see parts of His character.

I think so too! We have another word to learn today, Ben. Our next word is **consumer** (said this way: kŭn-soo-mer). A consumer isn't able to make their own food like a plant can. Instead, it needs to consume, or eat, food from a plant or animal.

Okay, so the mouse, snake, and hawk in our food chain are consumers, right?

Exactly right. Let's look at another food chain. This one starts with some grass.

The grass makes its own food through photosynthesis, so it is a producer!

Let's say a rabbit came along and enjoyed eating some of the grass. A few days later a fox catches the rabbit, and a few days after that a wolf catches the fox.

Okay, so we have a food chain of grass to rabbit to fox to wolf. The rabbit, fox, and wolf did not make their own food like the grass. They are consumers, right?

Yep! Let's practice identifying producers and consumers.

applyit Remember, a consumer cannot make its own food, but a producer can. Look at each picture, then circle producer or consumer to label what it is in the food chain.

producer   consumer

producer   consumer

producer   consumer

producer   consumer

producer   consumer

producer   consumer

Day

Hey, Hannah, I've been thinking about the food chain. It is interesting, but it also makes me feel sad for the animals. I don't like it when animals die.

I'm glad you told me. It makes me sad too. It's important that we go to the beginning of the Bible to find the reason. Let's read Genesis 1:29:

Then God said, "I am giving you every plant on the face of the whole earth that produces its own seeds. I am giving you every tree that has fruit with seeds in it" (NIRV).

Verse 30 also goes on to say that the animals and birds were given plants for food too.

So at the beginning, when the world was perfect before sin, people and all the animals only ate plants? The rabbit would have eaten only plants, along with the fox and wolf?

Right! But when Adam and Eve sinned, it broke God's original design. Some animals began to eat other animals. After the worldwide Flood in Noah's time, God told people in Genesis 9:3 that they could eat animals now too.

The effects of sin on the world do make us sad because we know it wasn't supposed to be like this. The food chain is a reminder that God's original, perfect design was broken by sin. We often see the sad effect of sin in creation. Romans 8:22 says,

We know that all that God created has been groaning. It is in pain as if it were giving birth to a child. The created world continues to groan even now (NIrV).

But there is good news! When we see the sad effects of sin, we also have hope because God has promised to restore creation someday. We'll talk more about that soon.

I'm looking forward to that! I think it is also important for us to watch for God's mercy as we continue to learn about the food chain.

God's original creation was perfect, but sin has sad results and it always destroys. Color the picture of the Garden of Eden. What do you think it might have been like there when all of the animals were friendly?

Read Genesis 3 together as a family.

This week was interesting, Hannah — but I have a feeling we have a lot more to learn about the food chain.

Oh, we sure do, so much more! But first, we need to record what we learned about this week. Scientists draw, sketch, and record the patterns they see in creation and what they've learned about so that they can share it with others.

We started learning about the food chain and how energy travels through it from the sun, to plants, to animals, and even people. We also learned that God's creation follows certain laws, and we see God's organization and wisdom in that.

I think we should draw a simple food chain in our Science Notebook this week!

Good idea! We can use the food chain picture from the first lesson this week to give us an idea. Or, you can ask your teacher to help you draw a different food chain. We'll show you our Notebooks, too. Let's have fun creating!

Ben, I like the rainbow-colored eagle in your Notebook!

Oh, thanks! I guess I was using my imagination a little too. Isn't Sam's gray snake cute? The food chain was fun to create!

In your Science Notebook, write: **A food chain shows us how energy moves through creation.**

Then, draw a food chain — and don't forget to tell someone about producers and consumers.

Hidden Treasure

The food chain reminds us that God's original, perfect creation was broken by sin. We see the sad effects of sin around us and through the food chain. Copy Romans 8:22 on the back of your Notebook page as a reminder.

We know that all that God created has been groaning. It is in pain as if it were giving birth to a child. The created world continues to groan even now (Romans 8:22; NIrV).

The Food Chain 2

Day

Ready to continue our science adventure this week as we look for God's design? I sure am! Last week we learned about producers and consumers. This week, we'll explore even more of the food chain. We have a few more words to learn first — these words will help us to organize and talk about consumers.

Remember, a consumer isn't able to make its own food like a plant. Instead, it must consume food from another plant or animal.

Some consumers only eat plants, some only eat animals, and some eat both plants and animals. We need a way to talk about and organize each type of consumer.

It's a good thing there are words to do that job! Our first new word for this week is **herbivore** (said this way: her-bĭh-vōr), and it means a consumer that only eats plants.

Hmm, so like elephants, deer, horses, and cows!

Our next new word for today is **carnivore** (said this way: kår-nĕ-vōr). This word means a consumer that only eats other animals. A lion, wolf, snake, and shark are all carnivores because they only eat other creatures.

Okay, so an herbivore only eats plants and a carnivore only eats meat. Our last word for today is **omnivore** (said this way: am-nĭh-vōr), and it means a consumer that eats both plants and other creatures.

Some types of birds eat seeds from plants and they also eat animals that have died. Raccoons and bears are also omnivores because they eat both plants and meat from other animals.

Remember that movie we watched about a bear, Ben? First, he enjoyed some blueberries and then he went to the stream to catch a fish for dinner.

Oh yeah! Omnivores like to eat a little of everything, while herbivores and carnivores are picky eaters — they only like one thing. Let's review these new words!

applyit Copy the meaning for each group of consumers.

Herbivore: a consumer that only eats plants.

Carnivore: a consumer that only eats fish or animals.

Omnivore: a consumer that eats both plants and other animals.

What is your favorite animal? Is it a herbivore, carnivore, or omnivore? If you're not sure, you can ask your teacher to help.

Alright, we learned about herbivores, carnivores, and omnivores yesterday — what's next?

Let's look at predators today. A **predator** (said this way: prĕ-dŭh-ter) is a consumer that kills and eats another creature.

So in our basic food chain with the mouse, snake, and hawk, the snake is a predator because it will kill and eat the mouse?

Yes. The mouse is the natural **prey** (said this way: prāy) of the snake. The hawk is also a predator because it will eat the snake.

What would be the predator of the hawk though? Shouldn't the food chain just keep going?

The hawk actually doesn't have a natural predator that would kill and eat it. The hawk is at the very top of the food chain, and we call it the **apex predator** (said this way: āpĕx prĕ-dŭh-ter).

Hmm, what about this — let's say a deer eats some grass. Later on, a wolf kills and eats the deer. A wolf is a predator. Is that the end of this food chain?

It is. The wolf doesn't have a natural predator. It is at the top of the food chain as the apex predator. Other examples of apex predators are lions, tigers, crocodiles, polar bears, orcas, and the great white shark.

Wait, there are food chains in the ocean too?

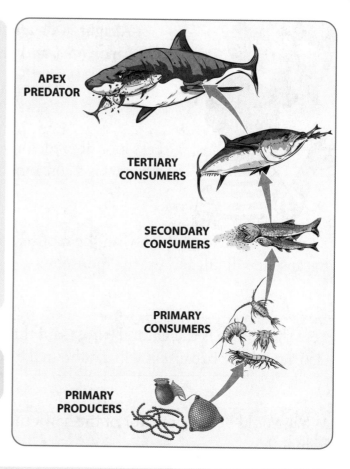

APEX PREDATOR

TERTIARY CONSUMERS

SECONDARY CONSUMERS

PRIMARY CONSUMERS

PRIMARY PRODUCERS

There sure are! But we're studying the boreal forest right now, so we're going to focus on the food chains in this biome. Let's make our own example food chain today!

apply it

Let's create a paper food chain. We can use a food chain from Yellowstone National Park. An elk is an herbivore — it eats plants. Elk are part of the deer family, and they are very large. Many elk live at Yellowstone, and wolves are their predator.

Our food chain begins with the sun, which gives energy to the grass. The elk can then eat the grass, and the wolf will hunt the elk.

To put together the food chain:

1. Cut out each part of the chain.

2. Put glue on the glue section of the sun strip, then attach the glue side to the bottom of the other side of this strip to create a circle.

3. Now, add glue to the glue section of the grass strip. Slip one end of the strip through the sun circle, then attach the grass ends to create another circle.

4. Repeat with the elk strip, and then with the wolf strip to create the chain.

Sun		Glue

Grass		Glue

Elk		Glue

Wolf		Glue

The elk is part of the deer family. You can learn more about deer in *God's Big Book of Animals*.

Blank for cutting.

Day ...

There is one more way we can organize the food chain. Let's learn about it today!

That sounds like a good plan. You must be talking about a trophic pyramid (said this way: trō-fĭk pēr-ĕh-mĭd). I read about it last night!

A trophic pyramid helps us to see the way many plants and animals are organized in the food chain, as well as how energy moves along it.

There sure is a lot of organizing in ecology!

That's because we see many relationships within ecology as we study. Organizing those relationships helps us learn and share them with others.

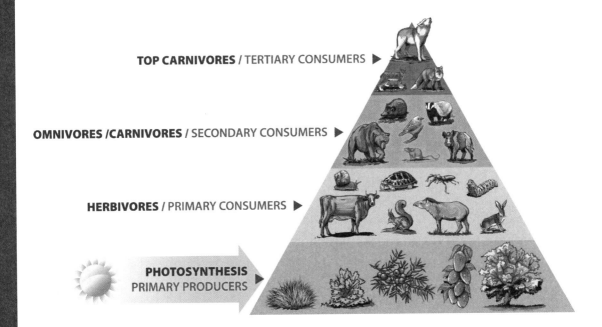

TOP CARNIVORES / TERTIARY CONSUMERS ▶

OMNIVORES /CARNIVORES / SECONDARY CONSUMERS ▶

HERBIVORES / PRIMARY CONSUMERS ▶

PHOTOSYNTHESIS
PRIMARY PRODUCERS ▶

At the base of the trophic pyramid are producers — these are plants. The next layer of the pyramid are the primary consumers. **Primary consumers** are herbivores — they only eat plants. Many types of animals and insects are primary consumers.

Producers form the base of the food chain, then there are primary consumers who only eat plants.

The third layer is made of omnivores and carnivores, and we call them **secondary consumers**. Secondary consumers can be the prey of an apex predator.

At the very top of the pyramid are tertiary consumers (said this way: ter-shē-āir-ē). Tertiary is a word that means third. An easy way to remember it is that these are the third layer of consumers on the pyramid. You'll find apex predators in this layer!

Whew, that's a lot to remember!

There is a lot of information, but it's easy to remember: producers form the base of the pyramid, and these are plants. The food chain starts with plants.

Now, what eats plants? Herbivores! Herbivores are the primary consumers. The next layer is secondary consumers, and these are carnivores and omnivores — but they aren't at the top of the food chain. Tertiary — the third group of consumers — are the carnivores at the very top. Let's color a trophic pyramid to help us remember!

apply it Color the trophic pyramid.

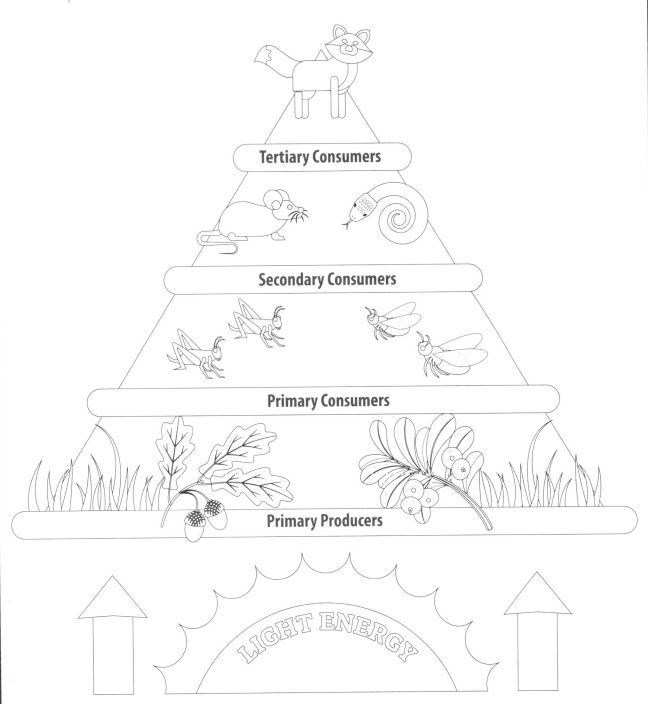

Tertiary Consumers

Secondary Consumers

Primary Consumers

Primary Producers

LIGHT ENERGY

We sure have learned a lot about the food chain! Next week we're going to look closer at the food chain in the boreal forest biome, right?

Yes! Now that we know more about the food chain, we're going to learn some really interesting history about the food chain in Yellowstone National Park. I can't wait to tell you all about it.

That sounds exciting! But Hannah, you mentioned last week that God will restore creation someday. Can we talk about that today?

Yes, we can! The Bible tells us that someday God will create a new heaven and a new earth. Sin and death will be gone forever, and creation will be perfect once more. Isaiah 11:6-7 tells us:

The wolf will live with the lamb, the leopard will lie down with the goat, the calf and the lion and the yearling together; and a little child will lead them.

The cow will feed with the bear, their young will lie down together, and the lion will eat straw like the ox.

Wow, what a day it will be when a wolf and lamb can live together! As we continue to explore the food chain, I'm going to remember that promise in Isaiah too.

applyit Draw a picture of what you imagine it will look like when wolves and lambs can live together peacefully.

It's my favorite day — the day we get to document what we learned about this week, just like a real scientist! Let's see, we talked a lot about different types of consumers and apex predators.

I think we should add an apex predator to our notebook this week!

Ooh, how about a wolf? The wolf reminds me of Isaiah 11:6.

Great idea! I have a couple of pictures here to help us get started.

The wolf is an apex predator.

We'll show you our Notebooks too. Remember to have fun creating! None of our drawings are perfect, but Ben, Sam, and I did our best and used the creativity God has given us.

We're going to show our grandparents when they come over for dinner tonight and tell them what we learned this week about carnivores, herbivores, omnivores, and apex predators!

notebook

In your Science Notebook, write:
The wolf is an apex predator.

Then, draw a picture of a wolf — and don't forget to tell someone about carnivores, herbivores, omnivores, apex predators, and God's plan to restore creation someday.

Hidden Treasure

Someday, God will restore creation, and the wolf will no longer be an apex predator. Copy the first half of Isaiah 11:6 on the back of your Notebook page as a reminder.

The wolf will live with the lamb, the leopard will lie down with the goat..." (Isaiah 11:6a).

A Broken Web

Day

Are we ready to explore the food chain at Yellowstone National Park? We've been learning about simple food chains, but each simple food chain in an environment is also connected to the others. Each chain depends on other chains to keep the ecosystem in balance. We call these connections the food web.

A food web shows how many plants, animals, and food chains are connected in an ecosystem like Yellowstone. Remember, ecology is all about relationships, and there are many relationships in the food chain.

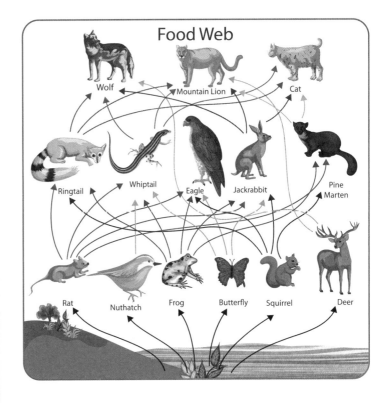

Food Web

Hmm, you said that each chain relies on other chains for balance — but there are so many links in the web. Would one link in the web being broken make a difference?

I'm glad you asked, Ben. There is really interesting history from Yellowstone that will answer your question.

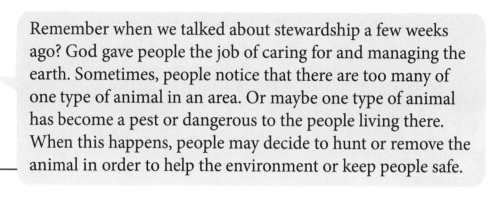

Remember when we talked about stewardship a few weeks ago? God gave people the job of caring for and managing the earth. Sometimes, people notice that there are too many of one type of animal in an area. Or maybe one type of animal has become a pest or dangerous to the people living there. When this happens, people may decide to hunt or remove the animal in order to help the environment or keep people safe.

As people moved around Yellowstone National Park in the 1800s, they thought the best thing to do to protect the environment and their cattle would be to hunt some of the big predators in the area like wolves and bears. But over time, too many wolves were hunted. Eventually, in 1926, there were no more wolves left in Yellowstone National Park.

Now, you might think that would be a good thing since wolves are an apex predator — but as the years went by, people began to realize that the wolves being gone actually made a difference in the ecosystem— a big one.

Hannah, Mom is calling us, so we better pause for today, but I can't wait to learn more of this history tomorrow!

apply it — Color the Forest Food Web image.

 You can learn more about wolves in *God's Big Book of Animals*.

I'm glad you're here, friend. I can't wait any longer to hear more of the story!

So by 1926, all of the wolves had been hunted out of Yellowstone, and it began to affect the ecosystem. The wolves hunted elk, which helped to keep the elk herds from becoming too big. Elk are herbivores, and they can eat around 20 pounds of plants each day.

When there were no longer any wolves to hunt them, the elk herds grew and grew. Over time, scientists believe the elk herds increased to well over 20,000 elk in the park!

Whoa, 20,000 elk eating 20 pounds of plants means they were eating around 400,000 pounds of plants each day! That must have had a big impact on the plants.

It sure did. The massive herds devoured the plants other animals relied upon. Elk enjoy eating young trees like willow, cottonwood, and aspen that grow in some areas of Yellowstone.

Those are all deciduous trees!

Beavers rely on these types of trees at Yellowstone National Park to build their dams. It wasn't long before the beavers had used up most of the tall, old trees — and then there was a problem!

There were now many elk, and they kept eating all the new, young trees. This meant that the trees weren't able to grow tall and strong for the beavers to use later on. Eventually, there weren't enough trees for the beavers to build and repair their dams with, so the beavers began to leave too.

Beavers are important because their dams keep calm, clean water built up in an area. This creates the perfect habitat for ducks and geese, as well as animals who have had their babies.

Without the beavers and their dams, these cool, calm streams began to disappear along with the habitats they gave to other animals. But the elk, willow, aspen, cottonwood, and beavers weren't the only things affected by the wolves being gone! We'll learn more tomorrow.

 **applyit**

A willow tree likes to grow in wet soil. They have branches that gracefully flow toward the ground and may even touch the ground. Aspen trees have white bark, and their leaves can turn beautiful shades of yellow in the fall. Cottonwood trees are tall and broad with rough, dark bark.

Below are images of an aspen, willow, and cottonwood. Use the descriptions above to identify and label each tree. Write an **A** for aspen, **W** for willow, and **C** for cottonwood.

_____

_____

_____

Beavers are amazing creatures! You can learn more about them in *God's Big Book of Animals*.

Day •••

Yesterday we learned that the wolves' being gone had a big impact on the elk herds at Yellowstone, which also affected deciduous trees and beavers. What else did it affect?

The elk were also eating up many of the wildflowers and bushes. This meant fewer seeds and berries for birds and even the bears.

No wolves also had an effect on the coyotes living there. Wolves do not like many coyotes in their territory, and they make sure only a few will be in the area. Without wolves around, the number of coyotes in Yellowstone also increased.

Just like the elk herds increased?

Exactly. Coyotes are not apex predators, though, they are secondary consumers. Coyotes often prey on animals like mice and rabbits. More coyotes meant that they were eating up more of the smaller animals that owls, hawks, and eagles also eat.

I think I can guess what happened next. Soon, there wasn't enough prey for the coyotes and the owls, hawks, and eagles?

You guessed it!

Wow, I didn't know all these food chains would be affected by wolves not being around! It affected so many parts of the food web when the wolves were not in Yellowstone anymore.

It definitely did. Wolves are a keystone species (said this way: kēē-stōne spē-shēz). A **keystone species** is a type of animal that the ecosystem depends upon. If a keystone species goes away, the ecosystem changes in ways we'll notice over time.

 When wolves disappeared from Yellowstone National Park, it impacted many plants and animals. Find these words in the word search below:

beaver   aspen   willow   mice   elk   coyote

B	E	A	V	E	R	Q	W	W	X	Z
P	M	N	V	B	E	M	I	C	E	K
V	X	K	M	Y	Z	S	L	D	F	J
R	A	S	P	E	N	E	L	I	B	E
L	S	V	Q	N	W	P	O	J	K	L
C	O	Y	O	T	E	L	W	M	P	K

 You can learn more about owls and mice in *God's Big Book of Animals*.

Day

In our fallen world, the food chain and even apex predators help maintain the balance in the environment. Without wolves, the elk population grew too big, which caused the deciduous trees and plants to dwindle. This meant that the beavers didn't have enough trees, and they began to leave Yellowstone. Once they left, the habitat the beaver's dam creates was also lost. Fewer plants and trees also meant less food for herbivores and omnivores — which impacted even the birds and bears.

It affected so much, Hannah! As we were reading this story it reminded me that creation is no longer perfect the way God originally designed it because of sin. But I think it is really amazing that God's mercy and wisdom still shows through the food web.

I thought wolves were a bad animal and the park would have been better without them! But they were actually important and helped to keep such a beautiful place and ecosystem balanced.

God knew what our imperfect world would need in order to maintain balance. Even in the death and destruction sin brought to the world, God designed creation in such a way that it could maintain balance so that many diverse species of birds, plants, and animals can live together in an ecosystem.

Colossians 1:16-17 says,

For in him all things were created: things in heaven and on earth, visible and invisible, whether thrones or powers or rulers or authorities; all things have been created through him and for him. He is before all things, and in him all things hold together.

That is a good reminder. I have good news too — this isn't the end of the story! Next week we'll learn how wolves returned to Yellowstone National Park and what happened when they were brought back in.

We learned some really neat history from Yellowstone National Park this week, and it's time to document what we learned. Hannah, what do you think we should draw in our Science Notebook this week?

Hmm, well we talked quite a bit about beavers and deciduous trees. Let's draw a beaver in our Notebooks! If you want, you can draw a stream and some deciduous trees too. Here is a simple beaver sketch we can use for an idea.

Oh, and here is a stream with a beaver dam if you'd like to draw that too!

Here are our Notebooks! I drew a family of beavers.

notebook

In your Science Notebook, write: **Beaver dams create an important habitat.**

Then, draw a picture of a beaver.

Hidden Treasure

Even in the death and destruction sin brought to the world, God designed creation in such a way that it could maintain balance so that many diverse species of birds, plants, and animals can live together in an ecosystem. Colossians 1:17 reminds us that God holds all things together. Copy this verse on the back of your Notebook page as a reminder.

He is before all things, and in him all things hold together (Colossians 1:17).

A Web Restored

Day !

Oh good, you're back to continue our adventure! I've been so excited to learn what happened when the wolves came back to Yellowstone. Are you ready, Hannah?

Ready! As time passed, people began to notice the effects of wolves being gone. They began to talk about the problems they were seeing at Yellowstone and argued about what to do.

Some people thought wolves should be captured from other areas and brought to Yellowstone to live there instead. Others were worried that wolves would be dangerous for the people who lived there. The ranchers worried that wolves would come and kill their cattle and sheep. Some worried that wolves would reduce the number of elk too far.

It doesn't sound like it was an easy decision.

It wasn't. There was a lot of debate. As stewards of God's creation, we manage, look after, and care for the ecosystems of the earth. Sometimes we don't know the best way to do that, though, and we make mistakes.

True, people thought at first that it would be better to remove the big predators like wolves from the park. But then they began to see that it wasn't really the best way forward.

Eventually people made a decision: since people had removed wolves from the ecosystem, it was also their job to bring them back. It's going to be fun to hear how the wolves were brought back!

applyit — Imagine you are at a meeting discussing whether or not to bring wolves back to Yellowstone National Park. Do you think you would be for or against bringing the wolves back? Think of the reasons why you are for or against the wolves coming back, and then tell your teacher why you think wolves should or should not be brought back to Yellowstone National Park.

Last time we learned that people decided that it was time to bring the wolves back into Yellowstone National Park. How did they do it?

Well, it took some time and very careful planning. People decided to capture wolves in areas where elk are their natural prey. The first batch of wolves were captured in Alberta, Canada. After the wolves were captured, radio collars were put on them so they could be tracked later on in the park. Then, the wolves were brought to Yellowstone. On January 12, 1995, the first eight wolves arrived!

Hurray! So on that day they just let the wolves run wild in the park?

Well, not exactly. First, the wolves needed to get used to their new environment, so they were kept together in a large pen. A few days later, on January 19, another group of six wolves arrived and began to get used to their new environment too.

Did people get to come and see the wolves like we do at the zoo? It would have been really neat to see those fourteen wolves!

No, people weren't able to go and see these wolves because they needed to be released back into the wild. The wolves' caretakers did their best to stay hidden so the wolves didn't get used to having people around.

Oh, that is a good point. It wouldn't have been good if the wolves got used to people being around and caring for them.

Once the wolves were ready, they were released into the park and monitored. Over time, things began to change at the park — we'll talk about those changes tomorrow!

 Color the picture of the wolf.

How did the park begin to change after the wolves were brought back? Did things go back to normal right away?

No, it did take some time for things at the park to begin to return to normal. First, the wolves were released, and they began to hunt the elk. The numbers of elk began to be reduced by the wolves. A drought also happened, which helped to reduce the number of elk even more.

What is a drought?

A **drought** (said this way: drŏwt) is a period of time when rain doesn't fall or not enough of it falls. Without rain, the soil dries out, which makes it tough for plants to grow. This meant the elk didn't have enough to eat.

Got it, so the wolves were hunting the elk, and the drought also helped because there weren't enough plants for the large herds of elk.

Once the drought was over, there were fewer elk to eat the plants and trees. Healthy aspen, willow, and cottonwood trees began to grow tall again in some areas of the park.

Did that draw the beavers back into the park?

It did. They began to build new dams, which also brought back an important habitat to the area.

What about the coyotes?

Wolves don't like coyotes in their territory, so the wolves also forced their numbers down. This meant more small prey was available for foxes, owls, and hawks. Which. . . .

Which meant more of those at the park!

It took many years for these changes to begin to be seen, and other things like the drought also helped bring balance back to the Yellowstone ecosystem. Today, around 100 wolves roam Yellowstone National Park, and there are around 8,000 elk.

What a difference! I'm glad we got to hear about that history, Hannah; it was really interesting!

You can read more about the red fox in *God's Big Book of Animals*.

The history we learned was all so interesting. I didn't know wolves could make such a difference in the food web!

Scientists and ecologists continue to study the impact wolves have on the park and the food web. They also study how the ecosystem continues to adjust over time. Yellowstone is a beautiful place, with many amazing ecosystems. I hope you're able to explore the area more with your family!

Ben, do you remember how we talked about God's glory in church? Glory is a word that means fame or renown. It's also a word that reflects our praise for God. There are lots of verses in the Bible that talk about God's glory. When I learned about this history from Yellowstone, it reminded me of God's glory.

It is amazing that God made creation perfectly — but He also gave it the ability to continue living even in an imperfect state. In our imperfect world, the food web keeps creation balanced and allows many species of birds, plants, and animals to exist together in an ecosystem. Each relationship within creation, big or small, proclaims the glory of God and His incredible wisdom.

And don't forget, even the sad parts like sickness and death brought by sin remind us of God's ultimate plan to restore creation someday. I look forward to that.

King David wrote about the glory and majesty of God that he saw in creation. When we look for God's glory and majesty in creation, we find it all over! In Psalm 8:9, David wrote,

Lord, our Lord, how majestic is your name in all the earth!

I'm excited to look for more glimpses of God's glory and majesty in creation as we continue our mission, Hannah!

Read Psalm 8 as a family.

Day

Well, it's time to wrap up our study for this week! Let's add a new page to our Science Notebook.

I'm ready, Hannah! I thought it was really neat to learn about the food web and how it maintains balance in our imperfect world. What do you think we should draw today?

Hmm, well, we are wrapping up our study of Yellowstone National Park, so I think it would be fun to draw a view from the park!

Oh, I like that! Here is an image we can use to give us an idea! If you have a book with pictures from Yellowstone, you can choose an image from that instead Earth you'd like.

Here are our Notebooks! We can't wait to see yours.

notebook

In your Science Notebook, write: **There is a beautiful ecosystem at Yellowstone National Park.**

Then, draw a picture of Yellowstone National Park.

 **Hidden Treasure**

Each relationship within creation, big or small, proclaims the glory, majesty, and incredible wisdom of God. Copy Psalm 8:9 on the back of your Notebook page as a reminder.

LORD, our LORD, how majestic is your name in all the earth (Psalm 8:9)!

Boreal Biome Project

Day

It has been so much fun learning about the boreal forest biome with you over the last several weeks! But I was reading about the deciduous forest last night — there are some amazing elements of God's design in that biome too. Do you think we could explore deeper into another biome now?

We sure can! There is so much more to study in other biomes, and many more elements of God's design to discover through ecology. First though, I have a surprise for you. We're going to create our own model boreal forest biome this week!

Woohoo! I'm so excited, where do we start?

First, we'll need a shoebox. Then we can start with the sky. I have some blue paper we can cut to fit inside the shoebox. I also noticed that there are mountains in the background of many pictures from Yellowstone. Let's add some mountains too! Are you ready to create a biome with us, friend?

Green, blue & brown construction paper	✓
Glue stick	
Shoebox with lid	
Scissors	
White paint & brush	
Glitter glue	
1/8-inch wooden dowels (6–12 inches long)	
Tape	
Playdough or clay	
Small model animals	
Small twigs or toothpicks	

Weekly materials list

materials needed

- [ ] Blue & brown construction paper
- [ ] Glue stick
- [ ] White paint & brush
- [ ] Shoebox with lid
- [ ] Scissors
- [ ] Glitter glue

Today, we'll create the background for our biome. We'll add something new to the biome each day this week.

Activity directions:

1. Ask your teacher to help you cut the blue piece of construction paper to the right size so that it can fit inside the bottom of your shoebox.

2. Now it's time to make the mountains! Cut medium-sized triangles from the brown construction paper. They'll need to fit on the blue piece of paper but should be large enough to stand tall in the background.

3. Paint the tops of the mountains white to make it look like there is snow on top. If you'd like, you can also add some glitter glue on top once the paint has dried.

4. Once the mountains have dried, glue them to the blue piece of paper.

5. Insert the blue piece of paper into the bottom of the box.

6. Set your biome in a safe place. We'll continue adding to it all week!

Hannah and I are all ready to make the land in our model biome today!

I'm so excited. I've been thinking about beaver dams — can we add a beaver dam to our model biome?

That's a great idea! Let's create some grassy land, and then add a pond with a little stream flowing from it. Then, we can add the beaver dam around the pond.

Perfect. I've gathered some small twigs we can use! Let's get started.

materials needed

- [ ] Green & blue construction paper
- [ ] Glue stick
- [ ] Hot glue gun
- [ ] Scissors
- [ ] Small twigs or toothpicks

Activity directions:

1. Tip your shoebox on its side (be sure the background is facing the right direction).

2. Cut the green piece of paper to fit inside the bottom.

3. Cut a circular pond out of the blue piece of paper, then cut a narrow stream. Glue both to the green piece of paper and set it inside the bottom of the model biome.

4. Now it's time to put together our beaver dam. Ask your teacher to use the hot glue gun to glue the sticks or toothpicks into the shape of a beaver dam. Be careful, the glue will be hot! You can also ask your teacher to glue some twigs upright to look like old trees the beaver can cut down.

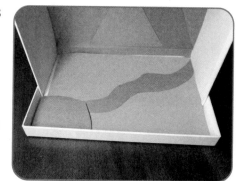

5. Set your biome in a safe place while the glue dries.

Alright, we've got our mountain background, the ground, and even a beaver dam in our model boreal biome. It's starting to look really good! What should we add today?

Let's add coniferous trees. After all, they are the main type of tree in this biome! I've got a plan to create some coniferous trees. Ready to get started?

materials needed

- [ ] Green construction paper
- [ ] 1/8-inch wooden dowels (6–12 inches long)
- [ ] Tape
- [ ] Scissors
- [ ] Playdough or clay

Activity directions:

1. Decide how many trees you'd like to add to your biome — 3–6 are recommended, depending on the size of your box. Remember to save room for deciduous trees and animals. Then, ask your teacher to cut or break the wooden dowels to the height you would like your trees to be.

2. With your teacher's help, cut 1-inch wide strips from the sheet of construction paper. Cut one strip for each tree you plan to make.

3. Carefully cut fringe in the paper strips — your teacher may need to help. You'll want each cut to go almost to the edge of the paper strip. Here's what it will look like:

4. Place the wooden dowel at one end of the paper strip. You'll want the paper to be near the bottom of the dowel. Tape the dowel to the paper edge.

5. Begin to roll the paper around the dowel at an angle, so that the paper begins to wind up the dowel. Once you reach the top, tape the paper to secure it. If the paper strip is too long you can cut it. Fluff out the paper fringe. You've created a coniferous tree! Repeat as desired to create more trees.

6. Form a small piece of playdough into a ball and flatten the bottom a bit. Insert the bottom of the dowel into the playdough. This will be the stand that holds the pine tree.

7. Place your coniferous trees in the biome and then put the biome in a safe place until tomorrow.

Day

Our biome is coming along. We're almost done!

I can't wait to see it tomorrow when we finish everything. Our coniferous trees look so good. The boreal forest is made up of mostly coniferous trees. But we also learned that sometimes we find trees like aspen, willow, or cottonwood around too.

Do you think we should add one or two deciduous trees?

I think so! We can cut some paper into the shape of a deciduous tree and tape it to the dowel, just like we did with the coniferous trees. Let's make yellow aspen trees for our biome!

materials needed

- [ ] Green or yellow construction paper
- [ ] 1/8-inch wooden dowels (6–12 inches long)
- [ ] Tape
- [ ] Scissors
- [ ] Playdough or clay

Activity directions:

1. Carefully cut one or two tree shapes from the construction paper.

2. Ask your teacher to cut or break the wooden dowels to the height you would like your trees to be.

3. Place the dowel in the middle of the piece you cut from the construction paper and tape the dowel to the paper.

4. Form a small piece of playdough into a ball and flatten the bottom a bit. Insert the bottom of the dowel into the playdough to hold your tree upright.

5. Add the trees to the biome and put it in a safe place — we'll finish off our biome tomorrow.

Day

Today is the day! We'll finish up our biome by adding some animals to it.

We have some small, model animals that we are going to put into our biome. If you don't have any, you can also use playdough to create some or ask your teacher to help you find and print some pictures you can use.

We also have some coniferous trees around our house. I cut a couple of small pieces off the branch for us to add to our biome. If you have coniferous trees around your house, you can add a small piece of a branch and pine needles to the floor of your biome, or even a small pinecone!

materials needed

☐ Small model animals such as a beaver, wolf, elk or moose, bear, rabbit, etc.

Activity directions:

1. Add the small animals to your boreal biome model.

2. If you have coniferous trees where you live, you can also add a small branch to your biome if you'd like!

3. Share your biome with your family. Be sure to tell them what you've learned about the boreal forest and God's design.

Bonus! Take a picture of your boreal biome and ask your teacher to help you print it out. Then, tape or glue the picture on the next page in your Science Notebook. Write **My Boreal Biome** at the top of the page.

Temperate Deciduous Forest

Day

Hello there, friend, I'm glad you're here! I hope you had fun exploring the boreal biome with us. We're excited to begin exploring the temperate (said this way: těm-per-ĭt) deciduous forest today. Be sure to keep your eyes open for God's amazing design as we learn! Where do you think we should start, Ben?

As we know, the word deciduous means trees that lose their leaves in the fall. While the boreal forest is made mostly of coniferous trees, the deciduous forest is made mainly of trees that will lose their leaves before winter.

That is an easy way to remember the difference between the boreal and the deciduous forest. Can you tell us what the word temperate means?

Temperate is a word that means mild or not extreme. When we put all the words together, the temperate deciduous forest is a biome that contains many deciduous trees and does not have an extreme climate.

Neat! Let's explore the climate deeper tomorrow. In the meantime, the temperate deciduous forest biome is the second-largest biome on land. We can find this biome covering some parts of Europe and Asia, as well as much of the eastern part of the United States.

Ooh, remember when we drove to New York to visit Grandpa and Grandma in the fall? We drove through many of the eastern states to get there. I remember that the leaves on the deciduous trees were such beautiful shades of red, orange, and yellow. Now I wonder, what makes those leaves change colors?

That was a fun trip, and we'll learn about why the leaves change colors in a few days.

 We're excited to explore the temperate deciduous forest with you! Let's copy this definition:

The temperate deciduous forest is a biome that contains many deciduous trees and does not have an extreme climate.

 Do you live in an area with deciduous trees, or have you ever traveled somewhere that does?

I read about the climate of the deciduous forest last night. I'm excited to share what I learned with you. While the temperate deciduous forest does not have an extreme climate like the boreal forest, it does go through all four seasons.

Hmm, so that means there will be some warm and hot days, as well as some cool and even cold days?

Yep! The climate can be cold in the winter and hot in the summer. But it is still mild when we compare it to other more extreme biomes like the boreal forest.

Interesting! So, what are the temperatures like?

Well, just like the boreal biome, the deciduous forest biome is also found around the world. This means the temperatures can be a bit different from place to place, but the average temperature over the course of a year is about 50° Fahrenheit (said this way: fair-ĕn-hīt).

In the summer, the temperature can be around 70–80° Fahrenheit. On the hottest days, it can even reach 90° Fahrenheit, but this doesn't happen very often. The deciduous forest usually receives between 30 to 60 inches of rain each year. Only the tropical rainforest biome receives more rain than that. We'll learn about the rainforest biome next!

During the winter, some areas of the deciduous forest may also receive several feet of snow. Winter temperatures can fall below 32° Fahrenheit, which is the temperature water freezes at.

Thanks for sharing, Ben! It sounds like the deciduous forest has a pleasant climate. Let's talk about the creatures we find in this biome tomorrow!

applyit Read each sentence below, then circle the phrase that will make the sentence true.

1. The temperate deciduous forest **has / does not have** an extreme climate.

2. The temperate deciduous forest has **four / two** seasons.

3. The temperate deciduous forest usually receives only **10-15 / 30-60** inches of rain a year.

 Ask your teacher to help you find the average rainfall or snowfall where you live.

Day • • •

I have a feeling we're going to have a lot to explore in the temperate deciduous forest! I learned last night that because the climate in this biome is mild, there are many types of plants, insects, birds, and animals that can live in this biome. The temperate deciduous forest is home to a diverse number of species.

What does a diverse number of species mean?

Let's look closer at those words! **Diverse** (said this way: dī-verse) is a word that means there is a lot of variety or different kinds. For example, when we visit the zoo, we see a variety of animals like monkeys, zebras, lions, bears, wolves, and many more. The animals at the zoo are diverse.

Species (said this way: spē-shēēz) is a word that means a kind of animal, bird, plant, or insect. Some examples of animal species would be gorillas, lions, dogs, squirrels, and raccoons.

Just like in the boreal biome, we'll sometimes find wolves, coyotes, and bears in the deciduous forest. Whitetail deer are also a common species here, along with raccoons, rabbits, skunks, foxes, and opossums.

But that's not all — there are many more species in this biome! There is also a diverse number of birds, from the common sparrow to the bright red cardinal, to yellow finches, and even to the strong eagle and owl. If you're able to walk through a deciduous forest, you may hear the beautiful sound of many birds chirping and singing in the branches above.

I love listening to the birds in our yard sing. That reminds me, we need to fill up our bird feeder!

applyit Let's complete a word search while Ben fills up the bird feeder. See if you can find these animal kinds in the word search below:

raccoon   skunk   fox   bear   opossum   deer   squirrel

R	A	C	C	O	O	N	Z	Q	P	M
W	C	X	J	K	K	D	B	E	A	R
L	J	K	N	T	R	E	W	D	H	L
S	Q	U	I	R	R	E	L	F	O	X
Q	K	V	Y	K	W	R	O	J	K	Q
S	O	R	O	P	O	S	S	U	M	P

You can learn more about raccoons, skunks, and squirrels in *God's Big Book of Animals*.

Hey, Ben, yesterday we learned that opossums live in the temperate deciduous forest. I read about them last night in *God's Big Book of Animals*. They are really interesting creatures!

When there is danger, like a predator near, the opossum will lay down and pretend to be dead. It can pretend so well that you won't even be able to see it breathing. Usually, a predator is not interested in a dead animal. When it is safe again the opossum will jump up and run away as fast as it can.

Wow! That is a neat way God gave them to protect themselves from danger.

It is! No one teaches the opossum how to play dead so well. God programmed this into them. We call that instinct! Instinct is something an animal just knows how to do — like how a bird just knows how to build a nest. No one tells the bird how or teaches it, the bird just knows.

God gave animals instincts so that they would know how to live and survive even in our imperfect world. For the opossum, their pretend death keeps them safe so that they can continue living the life they were designed to live.

Did you know that as followers of God, we also die so that we can live? When we put our trust in Jesus Christ, the Bible tells us that we die to ourselves — the part of us that chooses our own ways and sin — and we live instead for Christ. In Romans 6:11, the Bible says,

In the same way, count yourselves dead to sin but alive to God in Christ Jesus.

Thanks for sharing that, Hannah! I didn't know the opossum would give us such a good reminder!

DIGGING DEEPER

You can learn more about opossums in *God's Big Book of Animals*.

I'm ready to add a new page to our Science Notebook today! This week we started exploring the temperate deciduous forest.

My favorite part was talking about the instincts God gave animals. I see His design in that. Instincts help animals survive and thrive — even in our fallen world. The instinct God gave opossums to protect themselves is amazing! Can we draw an opossum in our Notebook?

I think that is a great idea! Here is an image we can use as an example. I'm excited to see how all of our opossums turn out! I love how each of our drawings are always different, and they always show the creativity God has given us.

Here is how our Notebooks turned out! I love Sam's colorful opossum.

In your Science Notebook, write: **The opossum lives in the temperate deciduous forest.**

Then, draw a picture of an opossum.

We learned about the temperate deciduous forest this week, and we also learned a little about opossums. Opossums pretend they are dead so that they can stay safe from danger and continue living. That reminded us of how we also die to sin so that we can live alive in Jesus. Write Romans 6:11 on the back of the page as a reminder:

In the same way, count yourselves dead to sin but alive to God in Christ Jesus (Romans 6:11).

Deciduous Trees

Day

Oh good, you're here! Ben and I were talking about deciduous trees last night. We'd like to learn more about them!

Let's start by comparing coniferous and deciduous trees. First, deciduous trees have leaves instead of needles. The broad leaves on a deciduous tree contain chlorophyll, just like pine needles. The broad leaves also give the deciduous forest another name — it is sometimes called a broadleaf forest.

Don't forget, chlorophyll is what the leaves and needles use to photosynthesize. Now, back to those leaves! Deciduous trees lose their leaves, usually before the cold weather of winter arrives.

How do the leaves know when it's time to fall off the tree? After all, trees don't have a brain like we do!

Good question! Summer days are long and hot. As the season begins to change to fall, though, the days become shorter and cooler. Shorter days also means there is not as much sunlight for the trees. This change in the amount of light causes trees to begin preparing for the winter.

Water is often frozen during the long winter months. This can make water hard to receive, so deciduous trees must protect the water they have inside themselves. Deciduous leaves do not have the thick, waxy coating that needles have to keep water from evaporating away. So, the deciduous tree loses its leaves to protect itself for winter.

That makes sense! How does the tree tell the leaves it's time to go?

Remember when you fell the other day and scraped your elbow? A scab formed over the scrape to seal and protect it. Deciduous trees work a bit like that too. When it's time for the leaves to fall from the tree, the branch seals itself off from the leaf. The seal between the branch and the leaf is kind of like how a scab seals the wound. Just as a scab keeps dirt and germs out of a cut, the seal prevents water and nutrients from flowing to the leaf. Eventually, this will cause the leaf to fall from the tree.

And the seal keeps water from being able to evaporate from the tree during the winter. I see God's design in that!

 Explain to your teacher or a sibling how deciduous trees lose their leaves.

I still have one question, Hannah. Why do the leaves on deciduous trees turn such beautiful colors in the fall?

As the days get shorter, the leaves stop making chlorophyll. Chlorophyll is green, and it's what gives the leaves their vibrant green color through the spring and summer. As the green chlorophyll fades from the leaf, other colors like red, orange, or yellow become visible.

Wow! I love seeing the bright, beautiful leaf colors in the fall. Have you ever noticed how leaves can look very different from one tree to another? I've seen some that are big, and others are small. Some leaves are also very detailed, but others are just simple.

That is true! There are many types of deciduous trees — like sugar maples, birch, elm, and aspen. Each leaf type can look a little different. Just look at all these leaves!

Each tree creates leaves that are unique to that kind of tree. While each tree type has a different leaf shape, there are some parts that are the same. Do you see the stem at the very end of each leaf? This is called the **petiole** (said this way: pĕt-ē-ōhl). The leaf is attached to the tree branch through the petiole.

Now, do you see the lines traveling through the leaves? These are called veins, and they carry water and sugar through the leaf. Look closer at each leaf and you'll see one larger vein that runs through the middle of the leaf. This is called the **midrib** (said this way: mĭd-rĭb).

What is the surface of the leaf called?

That is called the leaf blade. Let's see if we can identify the parts of a leaf!

applyit Write **P** for petiole, **M** for midrib, and **L** for leaf blade in the correct spaces.

If you have deciduous tree leaves around your house, see if you can identify the parts on one of the leaves.

We learned some parts of a leaf yesterday. Now that we know those, we can learn another easy way to identify different types of leaves. Ben read about this last night. Can you tell us what you learned?

I sure can! We can group, or classify, leaves into two types: simple and compound (said this way: kŏm-pŏwnd). A simple leaf is one whole leaf attached to the petiole. The leaves we looked at yesterday were all simple leaves. Can you see how the leaves are all one piece, attached to the petiole?

Ah, I see it! What about compound leaves? **Compound** is a word that means made of two or more parts. Does that mean compound leaves have more than one leaf?

You got it! A compound leaf has a thick petiole that many leaflets are connected to. Here is an example of a compound leaf. Can you see how each leaflet is attached to the thick petiole?

Thanks, Ben! So, a simple leaf is one whole leaf attached to the petiole, while a compound leaf has many leaflets attached to a thick petiole. Let's practice labeling simple and complex leaves.

 applyit Circle whether the leaf is a simple or compound type.

Simple Compound	Simple Compound	Simple Compound
Simple Compound	Simple Compound	Simple Compound

Learning how to identify leaves is fun and important because some plants are poisonous. Urushiol (said this way: oo-roo-shē-åwl) is a type of oil that the leaves of poison ivy, poison oak, and poison sumac contain. If you brush up against the leaves from one of these plants, the oil can cause an allergic reaction on your skin and give you an itchy rash.

poison ivy

poison oak

poison sumac

Day

I'm glad we spent some time learning more about deciduous trees this week! Isn't it interesting how God designed them to sense the days getting shorter and cooler? Because of this design they drop their leaves at just the right time.

God's wisdom is always incredible!

I've been thinking about the seasons. Each season is different and has something beautiful to offer. Our lives will go through the physical seasons of spring, summer, fall, and winter, but they'll also go through other seasons. Did you know we sometimes compare our lives to the seasons?

There are the seasons of childhood and becoming an adult. Sometimes, there are seasons of great happiness. Other times we may walk through a season of sadness. But no matter what season we walk through, God is still with us.

Right now, we are children. This is the season God has given us. We can trust Him with the future and enjoy the season we are in right now. In time, we will grow up and enter the season of being adults. Ecclesiastes 3:1 says,

There is a time for everything, and a season for every activity under the heavens.

It is fun to dream and look forward to things — but don't forget to enjoy the season you are in right now. Each of the four seasons and seasons in your life have good things to enjoy.

Read Ecclesiastes 3:1–8 as a family.

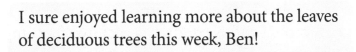 I sure enjoyed learning more about the leaves of deciduous trees this week, Ben!

Me too! What do you think we should draw in our Science Notebooks this week?

Hmm, let's draw a simple leaf and a compound leaf. I have a couple pictures we can use to help us!

Perfect! I really like how our Science Notebooks help us remember what we have learned and help us share with others. Let's be sure to label our leaves simple and compound.

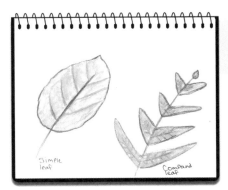

Here are our leaves. We can't wait to see yours!

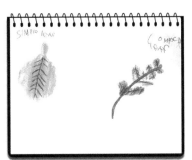

In your Notebook, draw a picture of a simple leaf. Then, label the picture **Simple Leaf**. Next, draw a picture of a compound leaf and label it **Compound Leaf**.

 Learning about deciduous trees and the seasons this week also reminded us that there is a time for everything in our lives. We can trust God with the season we are in right now. Copy Ecclesiastes 3:1 on the back of your Notebook page as a reminder.

There is a time for everything, and a season for every activity under the heavens (Ecclesiastes 3:1).

The Forest Canopy

Day 1

We had fun learning about the temperate deciduous forest's climate and deciduous trees. I'm ready to learn more about the forest itself now!

What are we waiting for? Let's get started! Ben, do you remember how we learned in *Adventures in Creation* that the ocean is divided into layers? The layers of the ocean help us to organize and talk about it.

Well, we can organize the forest into layers too. We call these layers the forest structure. The forest structure helps us organize and talk about the deciduous forest.

Organization is an important part of science, and it reminds us that God is also organized.

That is very true! Let's explore the layers of the forest, starting with the layer at the very top. The trees can grow quite tall and tower over the rest of the forest. We call this top layer of tall trees the forest canopy.

2 bowls	✓
Something to make your hand dirty. This could be mud, or something like yogurt or honey.	
Sink or bathtub	

Weekly materials list

The canopy is made of the deciduous trees that stand taller than the rest of the forest. The broad branches and leaves of these trees form a type of umbrella over the rest of the forest.

Hmm, that doesn't sound like a good thing. Wouldn't the umbrella of the canopy block sunlight from reaching deeper into the forest?

Yes, the upper part of the canopy will absorb most of the sunlight. But it also shields the forest from the harsh light and heat of the sun. Plants that grow beneath the canopy prefer shade. These plants would not be able to grow in the full light of the sun. The forest canopy gives other plants the shaded environment they need to thrive.

apply it The forest canopy is an important part of the deciduous biome. How does the canopy help to protect the plants underneath it?

In our last lesson we learned that the forest canopy protects the plants that grow below it. I wonder, does the canopy protect the forest in any other ways, Hannah?

It does! The canopy also shields the forest from storms — like an umbrella.

Ooh, remember that rainstorm we had a few days ago? The rain was falling so hard and fast, you couldn't even see to the end of our driveway! The rain also washed away some of the dirt in our yard.

We really needed an umbrella that day! The forest canopy shields the tender plants and animals from strong wind and rain, just like an umbrella shields us. When the raindrops fall hard and fast the leaves on the trees catch the raindrops. The leaves slow down the rain and spread out the raindrops. This causes the rain to trickle down gently to the forest floor.

The canopy also helps to protect the dirt and nutrients it contains. Strong rainstorms can cause the dirt to wash away, which removes nutrients from the environment. Because the canopy causes rain to slow down and spread out, it protects the soil in the deciduous forest.

Finally, strong storms can be very windy. The canopy helps to shield the forest from the strong winds of a storm. Sometimes, though, the strong wind may break a tree's branches, or even cause the tree to fall over. We'll talk more about what happens then in a few lessons.

Wow! Who knew the forest canopy had such an important role to play in the forest? The canopy impacts the environment and creatures all around it. God designed creation with so much wisdom! It's amazing to think about how parts of creation, like the forest canopy, impact other parts.

Activity directions:

The forest canopy is like an umbrella that shields the forest underneath it. Let's look at how an umbrella works today!

1. Turn the sink or bathtub faucet on full force and observe the strong flow of water.

2. Make the top of one of your hands dirty by spreading mud or something else on it.

3. Now place your dirty hand under the stream of water (make sure the water isn't hot!). The top of your hand should be under the stream. How quickly does the water wash away the dirt on your hand? Turn off the faucet.

4. Now, make the top of your hand dirty again. Turn the faucet back on and ask your teacher or a sibling to hold one bowl upside down under the stream of water. Then, hold the second bowl upside down underneath the first bowl. The second bowl should be slightly offset from the first bowl.

5. Put your hand under the flow of water coming down from the second bowl. Does the water wash your hand off as quickly this time or does it take longer?

The bowls worked like an umbrella and the forest canopy to slow down the water and spread it out. It took longer for the water to wash away the dirt on your hand the second time because the water was flowing gently. The forest canopy works in the same way to keep dirt and nutrients from washing away in the forest.

materials needed
☐ 2 bowls
☐ Something to make your hand dirty. This could be mud, or something like yogurt or honey.
☐ Sink or bathtub

I've been reading more about the forest canopy, and I wanted to share what I learned with you today. Did you know the canopy also helps to control the forest's temperature? I think that is really neat!

During the day, the canopy absorbs the harsh heat of the sun. This allows the forest to warm up slowly and not get too hot by the end of the day. At night, the broad branches help to hold heat within the forest.

Wow! So, the branches are kind of like the insulation in my winter jacket. My jacket helps to hold in the heat from my body so that I stay warm. The canopy impacts the deciduous forest in so many ways!

There are many deciduous trees that can be part of the forest. Some of the common types of trees are oak, birch, aspen, elm, beech, and maple. There are several types of maple trees too, but one really interesting type is the sugar maple.

That sounds like a sweet tree!

Oh, Ben, you're so funny! Do you remember our last trip to New York? We visited the sugar house with Grandpa and Grandma.

In the spring, sugar maples produce a clear, sweet sap. People drill holes in the tree trunk, then hammer a spout into the hole and hang a bucket underneath the spout. The sap will drain through the spout and into the bucket.

Oh, right! Then people will come through and empty the buckets of sap into a larger collection bucket.

It's a lot of work! Big maple farms use a system of hoses and tubes to carry the sap right to the sugar house to make the job easier and faster.

The sugar house is where they'll boil the sap. Boiling causes the water in the sap to evaporate which makes the sap into a thick, sweet syrup — maple syrup! I love maple syrup on my pancakes and waffles!

applyit There are many types of deciduous trees. Copy the name of each tree on the lines below.

oak   birch   aspen

elm **beech** **maple**

Ask your teacher to help you find a video showing how maple syrup is made. Real maple syrup can usually be purchased at a local grocery store. Plan a pancake or waffle dinner with your family and enjoy some sweet maple syrup on top!

What a fun week we've had exploring the forest canopy. I really enjoyed having waffles last night for dinner. Maple syrup is definitely one of my favorite treats!

Mine too! Some people make maple candy from the syrup too. Maple candy is so yummy! I'm glad God created the sugar maple tree. When I enjoy some sweet maple syrup, juicy grapes, or even crunchy carrots, it reminds me that God created many things we can enjoy. What do you enjoy most in God's creation?

Learning about the canopy this week and all the ways it protects the forest reminded me of God's protection over us. The forest canopy is like an umbrella or a shield over the forest beneath it. In the Bible, many verses talk about God as our shield, our protection, and our deliverer. King David wrote in Psalm 28:6–7:

Praise be to the LORD, for he has heard my cry for mercy. The LORD is my strength and my shield; my heart trusts in him, and he helps me. My heart leaps for joy, and with my song I praise him.

Our hearts can trust in the Lord; He is always our strength and our shield. I'm thankful for that, and it makes me want to praise the Lord just like King David!

Thanks for sharing, Hannah! That is a good verse to remember. That gives me an idea — let's memorize Psalm 28:6–7! We can create our own song to help us remember it.

Memorize Psalm 28:6–7 with your teacher. You can create your own song with the words to help you remember the verse. Sing your verse song to your family.

The forest canopy impacts the forest in many ways. It shields the plants underneath it from the strong heat and light of the sun. It protects the forest from the strong winds of storms and allows rain to fall gently to the ground. The canopy also helps keep the forest at the right temperature.

I see God's design in the upper structure of the forest. The tall deciduous trees protect the forest beneath them and provide a perfect habitat for many plants, insects, birds, and animals.

The forest canopy is made of tall deciduous trees. Let's draw a few deciduous trees in our Science Notebook this week! We can use these pictures for an idea. We'll show you how our notebooks turned out too.

In your Science Notebook, write: **The forest canopy protects the deciduous forest.**

Then, draw deciduous trees.

Learning about the forest canopy this week also reminded us that God is our strength and our shield. Copy Psalm 28:7 on the back of your Notebook page as a reminder.

The LORD is my strength and my shield; my heart trusts in him, and he helps me. My heart leaps for joy, and with my song I praise him (Psalm 28:7).

Under the Canopy

Day

We're ready to get started today! We've been exploring the temperate deciduous forest lately. In our last adventure, we learned about the forest canopy and all the ways it protects the forest. I'm excited to explore the second layer with you now! This layer is called the understory.

That's right! The understory is under the canopy. That is an easy way to remember where this layer is. What do we find growing in this layer, Ben?

The trees that stand tall in the canopy were not always so big and tall. They once started as small, young trees — and that is what we find in the understory.

These young trees grow slowly under the canopy until one of the tall trees dies or is broken by a storm. When that happens, sunlight reaches the young tree, and it will grow quickly in order to fill the space the older tree left behind.

I think it's neat how the younger trees wait patiently for a space to open for them. Then, once the time is right, they grow quickly to fill the space. This helps to keep the forest healthy.

Some trees actually don't like to receive full sun, and we find those types of trees growing in the understory as well. Since the canopy shields most of the sunlight, this creates the perfect environment for shade-loving trees. Do we find any creatures living in the understory, Hannah?

Oh, yes! Many forest creatures call the canopy and the understory home. You may find squirrels and chipmunks here, as well as owls and many types of insects. Many birds also build their nests in the understory.

 applyit Read each sentence below, then circle the phrase that will make the sentence true.

1. The canopy is **above / under** the understory.

2. Small, young trees grow **slowly / quickly** in the understory.

3. **Sun / Shade** loving trees grow in the understory.

 Wasp nests can often be found in trees or hanging on tree branches. You can learn more about wasps in *God's Big Book of Animals*.

Day

You know, we've been talking a lot about trees lately. We learned about different types of leaves, but I thought it would be fun to learn the parts of a tree too. I've been studying them so that I can share with you!

When we look at a tree, we see a thick trunk, branches, and leaves or needles. If we could look underneath the ground, though, we'd also see the many roots holding the tree firmly in place. The tree's roots may stretch deep under the soil, or they can be just a little way beneath the surface. The roots often stretch out wider than the tree's canopy.

When you look at a tree trunk, what is the first thing you see?

The bark! The bark provides a layer of protection for the tree, doesn't it?

Exactly! But did you know there is a second layer of bark underneath the bark you see? It is called the inner bark, or **phloem** (said this way: flō-ĕm). The phloem carries nutrients through the tree. But wait, before we go any further, we need to talk about cells.

Cells are what all living things are made of. Cells are extremely small, so we can't see them with our eyes alone.

The **cambium** (said this way: căm-bē-ŭm) is the next layer within the trunk. Its job is to create the cells that will cause the tree to grow. Underneath the cambium we find the **xylem** (said this way: zī-lŭhm). Xylem's job is to transport water through the tree.

Deep within the center of the tree is what we call the heartwood. The heartwood is made of tree cells that are no longer living like the cells in the other layers — but they will stay strong and give the tree the support it needs.

There are so many parts all working together for the good of the tree! Each part of the tree does a job and works together in relationship with the other parts to help the tree thrive. God's design in the tree is amazing!

 applyit Copy the name for each part of the tree trunk.

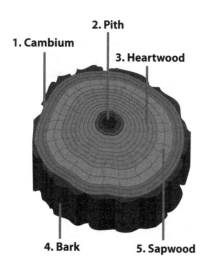

2. Pith

1. Cambium

3. Heartwood

4. Bark   5. Sapwood

1.

2.

3.

4.

5.

I enjoyed learning the inner parts of a tree trunk yesterday!

I'm glad; I thought it was interesting to learn about. I have one more thing to share with you, though — did you know that a tree also records how old it is?

No way!

It does! When a tree is cut down, we see many rings within the stump. The rings follow a pattern of light and dark. These rings reflect the growing season of the tree during the course of a year. We call them growth rings.

That is really interesting! How can we tell how old the tree is?

Well, the lighter color rings are usually formed when the tree grew quickly during the spring and summer. The dark color rings are usually formed as the tree grows slowly later in the year. By looking at a dark ring and the light ring next to it, we can see how much the tree grew during that year.

And if we count a dark and light ring as one year, we can add up how old the tree is through the rings! Hey, Dad cut down that old tree in the back yard a few weeks ago. The stump is still there. Let's go count the rings to find out how old the tree was!

apply it

How many rings can you count in this tree stump? Remember, a light and dark ring are counted as 1 year.

I counted _____ rings.

I'm glad we spent some time looking closely at the parts of a tree! It was fun to count the rings on that tree stump too. Let's talk more about the understory now. We haven't talked about the lower part of the understory yet! We often find shrubs in the lower part of the understory. Sometimes, this is called the shrub layer, but it can also be included as part of the understory.

What is a shrub? Is it a small tree?

No, a tree stands quite tall and has a wide trunk. A shrub is much smaller than a tree and has several wood stems that grow from the plant.

tree

shrub

Shrubs provide shelter for smaller animals like mice and chipmunks. They also often produce berries or seeds that are an important source of food for birds and other animals.

Let's review the forest structure. At the top is the forest canopy — this is made of the tall trees that shelter the forest. Under that, we find the understory. This layer has small and shade-loving trees. We also find the shrub layer here.

As we learned about the parts of a tree and how they all work together, it made me think of a passage of the Bible. God gives us each different gifts that we can use to serve Him — 1 Corinthians 12:4–6 tells us:

There are different kinds of gifts, but the same Spirit distributes them. There are different kinds of service, but the same LORD. There are different kinds of working, but in all of them and in everyone it is the same God at work.

The parts of a tree all work together for the good of the tree. Each job is important and needed. In the same way, God gives each of us different gifts, talents, and abilities. God uses all of them. The gifts you and I have are different, but it was God who gave us those different gifts. Each gift is important and needed as we work to serve God with others.

What is one way God has gifted you? Maybe you are really good at helping other people. Or maybe you love to sing and praise the Lord. Perhaps you love to cook or build things. How do you think God may be able to use your gift?

Day

What a week! We learned a bit about the understory and explored the parts of a tree. I'm excited to explore the last layer of the deciduous forest — but first, you know what time it is! It's time to add a new page to our Science Notebook.

I love drawing and sharing what we've learned. The best part is sharing my Science Notebook with others. It makes me feel like a real scientist!

Me too! I was thinking we could draw a tree and a shrub this week since they are both part of the understory. Remember, a tree has a wide trunk. A shrub is smaller and has many woody stems.

Great idea! I can't wait to see how your drawing looks. It's always a lot of fun to see how each of our Notebooks is different. We can use this image to give us an idea for what to draw for our shrub.

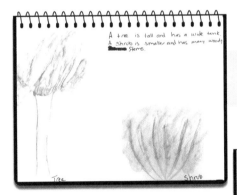

We can also draw the tree just like we did last week. Here's how our Notebooks turned out.

In your Science Notebook, write: **A tree is tall and has a wide trunk. A shrub is smaller and has many woody stems.**

Then, draw a picture of a tree and a shrub. Write **Tree** under the tree and **Shrub** under the shrub.

 Learning about the parts of a tree this week also reminded us that God gives each of us different gifts and abilities. Copy 1 Corinthians 12:4 on the back of your Notebook page as a reminder.

There are different kinds of gifts, but the same Spirit distributes them (1 Corinthians 12:4).

The Forest Floor

Day

We've been exploring the layers of the temperate deciduous forest, and we're almost through. Are you ready to explore the bottom layer? We call this layer the forest floor.

I'd say that the forest floor is the dirtiest floor you'll ever walk on!

Oh, Ben, you're so funny. But you're right, the forest floor is made of dirt and soil, as well as small plants and decaying material. Let's pause for a minute. Ben, what does the word decay mean?

Decay (said this way: dē-kā) means that something is breaking down. We also call this **decomposition** (said this way: dē-cŏm-pō-zǐ-shŭn). Decomposition is the process in which dead plants and animals break back down into the soil.

Thanks, Ben! We're going to be talking about decomposition quite a bit more as we explore. But first, let's learn a little more about the forest floor. It is a really interesting place.

Sounds good! What kinds of plants do we find growing on the forest floor?

Well, it depends some on where the forest is, but we often find plants like ferns, moss, wildflowers, and some types of grasses. We can also find fungus in the temperate deciduous forest.

Fun Gus? Oh, I love spending time with fun Uncle Gus! But what is he doing in the deciduous forest? I thought he lived in the city!

Oh, Ben, not our fun Uncle Gus. I'm talking about fungus. Fungus actually isn't a plant or an animal, it is its very own kind. Fungus is really interesting, and we'll be talking more about it soon.

Oh, okay, that makes more sense. Let's review all the layers of the forest together!

Write the correct name on each layer of the forest: **Canopy, Understory,** and **Forest Floor**.

We're back today to do some more exploring in the deciduous forest. Let's dig into the forest floor today! Can we start with the plants that grow there?

Sounds good! We can call the plants that grow on the forest floor the herb (said this way: urb) layer. This is where we find plants like beautiful wildflowers, graceful ferns, soft mosses, and tender grass.

Wait, I have a question. How can these plants grow if they don't receive very much sunlight?

Ah, I knew you would ask that question! In His wisdom, God created a large variety of plants and trees. Some need to receive full sunlight all the time, while others prefer shade. The plants that need sunlight create an umbrella of shade for the plants that prefer the shade. This allows many types of plants to grow together and create an ecosystem.

Neat! So, the plants that do need sunlight just don't grow on the forest floor?

Not quite. Some plants, like many flowers, need plenty of sunshine. In the forest, these plants are often the first to start growing in the spring. In fact, sometimes you can see their green stems popping up before the snow has even fully melted. These plants grow before the leaves on the trees so there is still plenty of sunlight reaching them on the forest floor.

Once the forest canopy has fully opened and shaded the forest, the plants have already grown and bloomed. The plant will die in the shade, but the roots will stay safe within the soil waiting for the next spring.

daffodils   tulips   trillium   bloodroot

Wow! God is a master designer. No one has to tell the plants when the right time to bloom is, they just do it! God designed them perfectly.

applyit Flowers that bloom quickly in the spring for a short time are called ephemeral (said this way: ĭh-fĕm-er-ŭhl) plants. Find the name of each ephemeral plant in the word search below:

daffodils   tulips   trillium   bloodroot

B	L	O	O	D	R	O	O	T	P	M
W	C	X	J	K	K	D	B	U	A	R
L	J	K	N	T	R	E	W	L	H	L
S	Q	U	T	R	I	L	L	I	U	M
Q	K	V	Y	K	W	R	O	P	K	Q
D	A	F	F	O	D	I	L	S	M	P

Day

Let's continue learning about the forest floor today! If we were able to walk through a forest together, we might find many fallen branches or even the trunk of an old tree on the forest floor. These provide habitats for small creatures and bugs.

If we looked closely at the ground, we would also notice a thick layer of old, dead plant and leaf debris. **Debris** (said this way: dě-brē) means the remains of something old, fallen, or broken.

The deciduous forest is full of deciduous trees. When all of the leaves fall off of these trees in the fall, it creates a thick layer of fallen leaf debris. We call it leaf litter.

Hmm, is it like the garbage litter we helped to clean up from the side of the road a few weeks ago? I didn't think littering was a good thing.

Littering with garbage isn't a good thing, but leaf litter actually does help the environment. When leaves fall from the tree to the ground, they begin to decompose.

Remember, **decompose** (said this way: dē-cŏm-pōz) is a word that means to break down into smaller parts.

The leaves break down into smaller and smaller parts over time. It can take one full year for leaves to completely break down. As leaves break down, nutrients return to the soil. Other plants can use the nutrients to continue growing.

If we were to take a rake into the forest in the fall and rake away the thick layer of leaves, we would find a crumbly layer underneath. The crumbly layer is made of old leaves and plants that have fully broken down. We call it humus, and it is rich in nutrients.

So the leaves and plants that die in the fall decompose during the rest of the year. As they do, they provide nutrients for the soil and other plants all year long. Do you see what I see, Hannah?

I think so! I see God's design. Not only are deciduous leaves beautiful in the fall, they also help to nurture other beautiful plants in the forest all year long.

 applyit Fall is a beautiful season. Color the fall leaves with bright orange, yellow, and red.

We've been learning about the forest floor together. We find small plants here in the herb layer, fallen leaves, and a layer of humus filled with nutrients for other plants. Is there anything else under the layer of humus?

Yes, under the humus we find other layers of soil or rocks. There could be sand or clay, depending on what area the forest grows. Nutrients from the humus layer will slowly sink deeper into the soil. Plant roots that grow deeper will be able to absorb the nutrients there as well.

The layers of the forest made me think of Romans 5:1–5. Let's read it together:

We have been made right with God because of our faith. Now we have peace with him because of our LORD Jesus Christ. Through faith in Jesus we have received God's grace. In that grace we stand. We are full of joy because we expect to share in God's glory. And that's not all. We are full of joy even when we suffer. We know that our suffering gives us the strength to go on. The strength to go on produces character. Character produces hope. And hope will never bring us shame. That's because God's love has been poured into our hearts. This happened through the Holy Spirit, who has been given to us (NIrV).

Did you notice the layers in that verse? It said that even when we suffer, we are full of joy. Joy is the feeling we have when we know everything is all right. Because of Jesus, we know that whatever is happening around us, we are always all right in His love.

When we suffer, we can have joy in Jesus. That suffering produces perseverance, or the strength to go on. The strength to go on produces character in us, and character produces hope. Suffering, perseverance, character, and hope layer upon each other and cause us to grow. As we grow, our lives look more like Christ.

I'm definitely going to think about that when I think about forest layers. Thanks for sharing, Hannah!

Termites are often found in the temperate deciduous forest. You can learn more about them in *God's Big Book of Animals*.

We have so much more to explore in the deciduous forest, I'm excited to continue our adventure!

Me too! But first, I want to document what we learned this week so that we can share it with someone else. I thought it was amazing how God designed some plants to bloom early in the spring before the forest canopy fills out.

God's design in that is amazing. I also see God's design in the fallen leaves. They provide nutrients for new plants in the forest all year long.

Let's draw the forest floor with some fall leaves this week. We can make the leaves colorful! Here is a picture we can use for an idea.

Great idea, Ben! Let's get started.

Here is what we drew in our Notebooks. I love all the bright colors in each of ours!

notebook

In your Science Notebook, write: **Leaf litter provides nutrients for the forest during the year.**

Then, draw a picture of the forest during the fall season.

Hidden Treasure

Learning about the layers of the forest also reminded us that suffering, perseverance, character, and hope layer upon each other and cause us to grow. As we grow, our lives look more like Christ. Copy Romans 5:3–4 on the back of your Notebook page as a reminder.

And that's not all. We are full of joy even when we suffer. We know that our suffering gives us the strength to go on. The strength to go on produces character. Character produces hope (Romans 5:3–4; NIrV).

Day Decomposition

Oh good, I'm glad we're all back together! We talked a little bit about decomposition in our last adventure. I was interested in learning more, so I've been reading all about it. I'm excited to share what I've learned with you!

I can't wait to hear what you've learned. Where do we start?

We learned before that decompose is a word that means to break down into smaller parts. But the material doesn't break down all by itself — decomposers help! A decomposer is something that works to decompose material.

Before we go any further, do you remember what we learned about the food chain?

Yes, the food chain shows how energy moves through creation.

There is one more part of the food chain that we haven't learned about yet. Decomposers are part of the food chain too! When a plant or animal dies, they still have energy available. Decomposers eat and break down dead material so that the energy can be used again.

Ooh, it's like recycling! We set aside plastic bottles so they can be recycled and turned into something new.

A ripe banana ✓

Plate ☐

Weekly materials list

Exactly! Decomposers recycle the old, dead material so that the energy can be used by new plants and animals. Without decomposers, energy would eventually get all tied up and nothing would be able to use it.

Wow! God is a master designer. Isn't it amazing how energy cycles through creation over and over? I'm interested in learning more about decomposers. What are they?

There are many different kinds of decomposers. A few types are fungi, bacteria, earthworms, flies, termites, and millipedes. We'll be talking more about a few of them!

I'm excited to learn more. First, though, now that we know decomposers are also part of the food chain, let's take another look at it!

The food chain shows how energy moves through creation. The food chain begins with producers. Remember, these are plants that can produce their own food. Primary consumers are next — these are herbivores that eat the plants.

Next come secondary consumers. These are carnivores and omnivores, but they aren't at the top of the food chain. Tertiary consumers are the consumers at the top of the food chain, and apex predators sit at the very top. Once an apex predator, or anything else, has died, decomposers work to decompose so that nutrients can be used again by producers. Study the image of the food chain on the next page, then explain to your teacher how energy moves through the chain.

Mice

Secondary Consumer

Snake

Tertiary Consumer

FOOD CHAIN

Grasshopper

Primary Consumer

Hawk

Apex Predator

Grass

Producer

Fungi

Decomposers

Day

Are we ready to learn more about decomposers? I've been studying fungus so that we can talk about it today! Like you mentioned before, fungus isn't an animal or a plant, it is its own kind of living thing.

We use the word fungus to talk about one type of fungus. We use the word fungi to talk about many types of fungus. One type of fungi are mushrooms, another type is yeast.

Ooh, we use yeast to make bread! It's what makes the bread rise taller.

Like an animal, fungi aren't able to make their own food. They need to consume food from something else. Yeast consumes the sugar in flour. As it eats, the yeast creates gases that cause the dough to rise. Other types of fungi, like mushrooms, consume material from dead plants or animals.

But I've looked at mushrooms before and they don't have mouths. How can they digest something else?

The fungus grows **hyphae** (said this way: hī-fŭh). Hyphae are kind of like roots that branch out and attach to the material the fungus will eat. The fungus will then use a special **enzyme** (said this way: ĕn-zīm). An enzyme is a substance that digests or breaks down another substance. The fungus' enzyme digests the material. The fungus will use some energy for itself, and the rest of the broken down material returns to the soil for another plant to use.

Cool! I've seen mushrooms before in the forest, but I didn't know they were doing such an important job.

 Find these words in the word search below:

fungi   hyphae   enzyme   mushroom   fungus   yeast

P	F	Z	Y	E	A	S	T	X	P	H
M	U	S	H	R	O	O	M	U	K	Y
K	N	F	J	L	M	N	W	Q	Z	P
X	G	K	L	Q	S	B	N	M	L	H
F	U	N	G	I	W	R	Z	P	K	A
J	S	K	Q	O	E	N	Z	Y	M	E

You can learn more about flies in *God's Big Book of Animals*.

Day ●●●

Bacteria is another type of decomposer I've been learning about. Let's talk about it today! Bacteria is all around us. It can be found on every part of the earth from the tops of the highest mountains to the deepest parts of the sea.

Wait, if bacteria are everywhere, how come I've never seen it?

Bacteria are actually too small to see with your eyes alone. Scientists study bacteria through a microscope. A microscope is a tool that makes very small things visible to our eyes.

Bacteria are very important in creation, even though they are too small for us to see. For example, bacteria actually cover our bodies and help to keep them healthy!

No way!

They do — we are covered in bacteria inside our bodies, as well as outside of our bodies. Bacteria are found everywhere! Many types of bacteria are helpful and work to keep our bodies healthy and balanced. This is another relationship in creation!

Bacteria can also work as a decomposer that helps to recycle energy. These types of bacteria work to decompose plant or animal material after it has died. We can't see bacteria working without a microscope, but we can observe their work over time. Hey, that gives me an idea — let's go get a banana and we can observe bacteria at work!

Activity directions:

materials needed

☐ A ripe banana

☐ Plate

1. Peel the banana, then place both the banana and the peel on the plate.

   Look at the banana and peel. Then, answer these questions:

   What does the banana look like?

   Does the banana look good to eat?

   What does the banana smell like?

2. Set the plate on the countertop. Bacteria will begin to slowly decompose the banana. Optional: take a picture so you can compare the banana later on.

3. Wait several hours, then look at the banana and the peel. Do you see any changes, or does it look and smell the same?

4. Look at the banana and peel the following afternoon. Then, answer these questions:

   What does the banana look like now?

Does the banana look good to eat?

What does the banana smell like now?

Bacteria has begun to decompose the banana, and it probably doesn't look or smell as good as it did yesterday! As more time goes on, the banana will rot and decompose further. Once you are done observing the banana be sure to discard it.

Another important decomposer is the earthworm. Earthworms may seem like simple creatures, but they are very important decomposers in their environment! Earthworms look a bit like tiny snakes, but you can't easily see their mouths. The earthworm's body has segments that look like rings. Earthworms use the segments to dig tunnels through the soil. As it tunnels, the earthworm eats the soil.

Soil doesn't sound like a great meal to me!

It isn't for us, but it is a nutritious meal for the earthworm! It digests nutrients that the plants can't use. An earthworm's tunnel also helps fresh air move through the soil which keeps the soil healthy. Once it has digested nutrients in the soil, the waste is released from the earthworm's body.

Wait, by waste do you mean poop?

Yes, earthworm poop is called castings. The castings are also full of nutrients — but now they are in a form that the plants can use. Earthworms help keep the forest soil healthy.

Wow, I didn't know worms were so important! Isn't it neat how decomposers can recycle nutrients for new plants and animals?

While decomposers can recycle material for new plants and animals, they can't make that old material alive again. However, when we trust in Jesus, He brings us from death to life in Him. In Romans 6:11–14, we read:

In the same way, consider yourselves to be dead as far as sin is concerned. Now you believe in Christ Jesus. So consider yourselves to be alive as far as God is concerned. So don't let sin rule your body, which is going to die. Don't obey its evil desires. Don't give any part of yourself to serve sin. Don't let any part of yourself be used to do evil. Instead, give yourselves to God. You have been brought from death to life. Sin will no longer control you like a master. That's because the law does not rule you. God's grace has set you free (NIrV).

I'm so glad that Jesus brings us from death to life and that sin no longer controls us like a master, aren't you?

Ask your teacher to help you find a time-lapse video online of earthworms decomposing material.

Day

Did you have fun exploring decomposers?

I sure did! We're going to explore forest habitats next, and I'm looking forward to that. But first, it's time to add another page to our Science Notebook!

Our Notebooks are really starting to fill up now. Isn't it fun to look back at the other pages and remember all the things we've learned so far?

And don't forget all the areas we've seen God's design in creation!

For sure. Let's see, we learned about decomposers this week. What if we draw an earthworm in our Notebook?

I like that idea! Here is a sketch we can use for an idea.

Here is what Ben, Sam, and I drew in our Notebooks!

Earthworms help keep the forest soil healthy.

EARTHWORMS help keep the forest soil healty

In your Science Notebook, write: **Earthworms help keep the forest soil healthy.**

Then, draw a picture of an earthworm.

 Learning about decomposers this week also reminded us that only God can bring us from death to life. It is His power that frees us from sin. Copy Romans 6:13b on the back of your Notebook page as a reminder.

You have been brought from death to life. So, give every part of yourself to God to do what is right (Romans 6:13b; NIrV).

Lichens

Day

We're almost done exploring the temperate deciduous forest! I'm looking forward to creating our own model biome soon. But before we do that, we still have a couple of things to explore here. We're going to learn about something really interesting today, but we need to learn some new words before we do. Let's start with the word organism. Can you tell us what this word means, Ben?

Absolutely! An **organism** (said this way: ōr-guh-nĭz-ŭm) is a living thing like a person, animal, plant, or even fungus.

Those are all great examples of organisms. Another organism is called algae (said this way: ăl-jē).

Oh, I've seen algae! It grows in our fish tank and makes the glass all green and slimy. We have to clean it out every now and again.

That's right! We've also seen algae growing in a pond. Remember that time you slipped and fell into the pond? You had green algae all over your hair!

I do remember. I wasn't happy about it!

No, you weren't! Anyway, we learned about fungus a few days ago. Fungus and algae are two different organisms. Do you think they have any relationship with each other?

Hmm, I wouldn't think so. But I've been surprised before! What is the relationship they have?

Fungus and algae have what is called a symbiotic relationship. A **symbiotic** (said this way: sĭm-bē-ŏt-ĭk) relationship means that the organisms live together in a close relationship. This is also called symbiosis (said this way: sĭm-bē-ōh-sĭs). We're going to be learning more about their relationship. Let's copy the meaning of the word symbiotic first, though!

 Copy the definition below.

A symbiotic relationship means that the organisms live together in a close relationship.

I'm all ready to learn more about this symbiotic relationship between fungus and algae. Can you tell us more about it, Hannah?

Let's get right to it! Just like a plant, algae can photosynthesize, which allows it to get energy from the sun. However, algae does not have a strong structure. It can't grow in many different environments all by itself.

On the other hand, fungus does have a strong structure that can grow in many places. However, it needs to be able to get energy.

Ooh! So, if algae and fungus form a relationship, fungus can give the algae structure, and the algae can give the fungus energy through photosynthesis!

You got it! When fungus and algae form a symbiotic relationship, we call the result a **lichen** (said this way: lī-kŭhn).

Lichens can grow in many environments and biomes. They can also look very different from one another, but there are three main shapes that we find. The first is called foliose (said this way: fō-lē-ōs). Foliose lichens look a bit like leafy lettuce or like the edges of shriveled up leaves.

The second type of lichen is called crustose (said this way: krŭs-tōs). These lichens can often be found on rocks, in the dirt, or even on a roof. They look like a colorful crust on top of something. The third type is called fruticose (said this way: froo-tĭ-kōs) lichens. Some stand tall and look like little cups, while others look more like a bush or a clump of hair.

apply it Spend some time exploring your environment. See if you can find any lichens growing in your area. Be sure to check any trees or rocks that you can find. Here are some lichens we found growing around us! If you cannot find any lichens, ask your teacher to help you look up images of lichens online.

Bonus! If you find lichens, ask your teacher to help you take a picture of what you found. Then, print out the picture and tape it into your Science Notebook. Write **Lichens** at the top of the page. Be sure to write the date and place you found them growing to record your discovery like a scientist!

The symbiotic relationship that forms lichens is really interesting! I can see how both fungus and algae receive a benefit from each other. We've also seen before how an organism or relationship impacts other parts of creation. Do lichens have an impact on anything else, Hannah?

They sure do! Remember when we talked about keystone species as we learned about Yellowstone National Park? These are species that have an important impact on the environment, and we would notice if they disappeared. Lichens are so important in many environments that they are often a keystone species!

Lichens impact the environment in which they live in many ways. They are an important part of the food chain. Lichens provide food and energy for many species that live in the deciduous forest. Birds also use lichens to help build their nests. Lichens help to protect the trees that they grow on. They also absorb water and nutrients that they can release again later when it is needed.

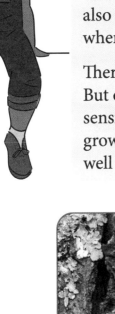

There are a few other ways lichens impact the environment. But one other interesting thing about them is that they are very sensitive to the air around them. Lichens absorb air, and they grow best when the air is fresh and clean. Lichens will not grow well at all when there is pollution in the air.

Pollution (said this way: pŭh-loo-shŭn) is a word that means something harmful has been released, or that something has been contaminated with something else. Let's imagine you have a clean, cool glass of milk in front of you. Before you take a sip, though, I dump a spoon of dirt into the cup.

Yuck!

Would you still want to drink the milk? I sure wouldn't because the clean milk has been polluted with dirt that shouldn't be there.

Good point, Ben! Pollution in the air can harm the people, plants, and animals that live there. Lichens help scientists monitor how clean and fresh the air is. If lichens in an area begin to stop growing or die, it is a sign that the air is becoming polluted.

applyit Write the missing word in each sentence:

food   pollution   keystone

1. Lichens are a _____ species.

2. Lichens are an important part of the _____ chain.

3. Lichens do not grow well when there is _____ in the air.

I'm glad we were able to learn more about lichens over the last few days! Isn't it neat to see how one relationship can affect so many other things?

It is! The symbiotic relationship between fungus and algae creates a food source, helps birds build their nests, protects trees, stores nutrients, and even helps us make sure the air around us stays clean.

Lichens remind me that relationships are important. Our relationships with each other are important too — and they will have an impact on those around us. In Matthew 22:36–39, we read,

"Teacher, which is the greatest commandment in the Law?" Jesus replied: " 'Love the Lord your God with all your heart and with all your soul and with all your mind.' This is the first and greatest commandment. And the second is like it: 'Love your neighbor as yourself.' "

Oh, I remember that verse. We talked about it in Sunday school. First, we must love God with all of our heart, mind, and soul. Then, we love and care for our neighbor just as we do for ourselves. Our neighbor is any person around us like our family, friends, and neighbors.

Our relationships have an impact on ourselves as well as others. We can have a good impact by loving as Jesus teaches us. Or we can also have a bad impact by not caring for others.

Sometimes it is hard to love and care for other people, especially when they don't treat us kindly. But I pray and ask for God's help. I want to have a good impact on the people around me and show them the love Jesus has shown me.

What are some ways you can love and care for the people around you?

I'm ready to share what we've learned about this week. That is a good thing because it's my favorite day — Science Notebook day! Lichens are a neat part of God's creation. I enjoyed learning about the impact God designed them to have on the environment. It was also fun looking around our house — we found some beautiful lichens I never knew were there before!

I enjoy looking around for lichens now! It's fun to see all the different places they grow. Let's draw some lichens in our Notebooks this week. We can use this image for an example. You can draw each type of lichen, or you can pick just one. If you found lichens around your home, you could also draw a picture of what you found instead.

Here is how each of our lichen drawings look. Have fun drawing yours!

Lichens help their environment.

Lichens help their environment

notebook

In your Science Notebook, write: **Lichens help their environment.**

Then, draw a picture of a lichen.

 **Hidden Treasure**

Learning about lichens this week reminded us that our relationships are important too. We can impact others for good or bad. Copy Matthew 22:37–39 on the back of your Notebook page as a reminder.

Jesus replied: " 'Love the Lord your God with all your heart and with all your soul and with all your mind.' This is the first and greatest commandment. And the second is like it: 'Love your neighbor as yourself' " (Matthew 22:37–39).

Forest Relationships

Day

Hello, friend, we're all ready to get started today! Since we've learned about lichens and the symbiotic relationship they have, I thought it would be fun to explore other relationships in the forest.

That does sound like fun! I'm guessing we'll need to learn some new words first.

We sure will! As we learned last time, a symbiotic relationship means that the organisms live together in a close relationship. But we can organize symbiotic relationships even further!

The first type of symbiotic relationship is called **mutualism** (said this way: myoo-choo-ŭh-lĭz-ŭhm). Mutualism is a symbiotic relationship in which two organisms receive a benefit from each other.

Like the lichens!

Right! Let me think of another example — a deer! Deer often live in the deciduous forest. One problem that wild animals, like deer, often have is that insects like to live in their fur. Insects can make the animal itchy.

They can also crawl around the deer's eyes and ears; I imagine that would get really annoying!

It sure would! A deer will allow a bird to come and eat the bugs off of it. The bird will come land on the deer and enjoy a good meal.

Neat! The deer gets rid of those pesky insects and the bird gets a full belly — they both benefit!

We also see mutualism between bees, butterflies, and flowers. The flowers have nectar that bees and butterflies eat. The flowers also need pollen from other flowers. Bees and butterflies land on the flowers to drink the nectar, and pollen from the flower sticks to their legs.

When the bee or butterfly lands on the next flower, some of the pollen will fall off their legs and onto this flower. So, the bee and butterfly receive food, and the flower's pollen is carried through the forest. They both receive a benefit through their relationship.

 applyit Copy the definition below.

Mutualism is a symbiotic relationship in which two organisms receive a benefit.

I'm here and ready to learn about the next type of relationship. Let's get started!

Alright! The second type of relationship is called commensalism. **Commensalism** (said this way: kŭh-mĕn-sŭh-lĭz-ŭhm) is a big word that means two organisms have a relationship, but only one receives a benefit. One important thing about commensalism is that the other organism isn't harmed.

Interesting. So one receives a benefit and the other isn't harmed. Let me think of an example of that. Birds! Birds build their nests in strong, safe trees. A bird receives shelter and protection from the tree, and the tree isn't hurt by the bird.

Before we learn the third type of relationship, we need to learn an extra word. A **parasite** (said this way: pair-ŭh-sīt) is an organism that lives inside or on a different organism and receives nutrients from it. The parasite receives the benefit, but it can also be harming the other organism. We call the other organism the host.

The third type of relationship is called **parasitism** (said this way: pair-ŭh-sĕh-tĭzm). Parasitism is a relationship when a parasite lives on a host.

That doesn't sound like the best kind of relationship to have!

It isn't a good relationship for the host! One type of parasite is a tick.

Ticks are not my favorite. Dad has had to pull a few off of my legs after we've gone hiking!

Ticks may bite onto animals like dogs and deer, or even people sometimes. The tick receives food from the host, but they don't have a benefit to give the host. Let's review the words we learned about today!

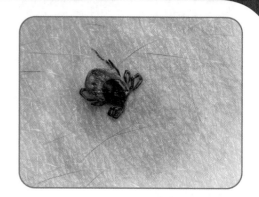

 apply it Let's practice. Can you match each word with the correct meaning?

Parasite

A type of relationship in which two organisms have a relationship, but only one receives a benefit.

Commensalism

An organism that lives inside or on a different organism and receives nutrients from it.

Parasitism

A relationship when a parasite lives on a host.

I've really enjoyed learning about different types of symbiotic relationships this week. I've also been thinking about what it would have been like when God first created the world. Everything was perfect then!

Very true. The relationships in the original creation may have looked different. But then sin entered the world and affected creation. Now we see sickness and death in an imperfect creation. It's a reminder that sin has sad consequences, but we have hope through Jesus!

And someday He will restore creation. I look forward to that! I thought it would be fun today to look at how different creatures live and interact in the deciduous forest. Let's take turns describing the forest.

Imagine we've been walking through a deciduous forest. It's fall; the air is fresh and crisp. The leaves that line the forest floor have been crunching under our shoes. We're tired from walking, so we sit down next to a fallen tree. Your turn, Hannah!

Hmm, as we sit, we hear the distant *caw, caw* of a crow. Suddenly, we notice the ground near the fallen tree is moving! When we look closer, we see an earthworm recycling the old leaves. Various beetles and ants also crawl from under the fallen tree trunk — it has created a good habitat for them.

Then, we hear a strange *plop, thunk* sound followed by the rustling of leaves. What could it be? As we look through the trees, we notice a squirrel skipping across the branches of an old oak tree. He is gathering acorns to store for food through the cold winter. Every now and again an acorn falls from his grasp and plops to the forest floor. In time it may grow into a new tree!

Wait, what is that in the distance? Look closely, it's a deer! It is walking gracefully through the forest. Just then, another strange sound rings out through the forest. It sounds like something hammering into wood very quickly.

We follow the sound and find the source! It's a black and white bird with a red cap on its head — a pileated woodpecker!

 Now it's your turn! Imagine what it would look, sound, and smell like as you walk through the deciduous forest. Describe the forest to a friend or family member.

You can learn more about the pileated woodpecker in *God's Big Book of Animals.*

Hasn't it been interesting to learn about a few different types of relationships we see in creation? I also enjoyed using our imaginations to describe the forest!

Me too! I've been thinking about parasitism since we learned about it, though. It's a pretty selfish type of relationship. The parasite only takes from the host. And sometimes, the parasite may carry a disease that will even harm the host. We talked about how our relationships impact others a few days ago. Parasitism reminded me of Philippians 2:3–4:

Do nothing out of selfish ambition or vain conceit. Rather, in humility value others above yourselves, not looking to your own interests but each of you to the interests of the others.

I've been thinking about how I can look out for others and care for them. I want to value others like the verse says.

I'm glad you shared with us, Ben! We're naturally selfish because of sin, but Jesus helps us to change. He teaches us how to look out for others and care for them. I pray and ask God to help me see ways I can love and serve the people around me.

Mom and Dad also help us learn how to value others. I want to grow up to be a person who values others, and I'm learning how to do that now with God's help.

applyit Helping others is one way we can value them. Draw a picture of you helping someone else.

Day

Next week we'll begin creating our own temperate deciduous biome! I'm really excited about that; I can't wait to finish it and show it to my friends!

You must be excited; it sounds like you forgot that today is the day we share what we learned in our Science Notebooks.

Oh, I didn't forget; I couldn't forget my favorite day! I've got my Science Notebook and colored pencils all ready to go! I was thinking about mutualism today. We could draw a bee and a flower to show this type of relationship!

Oh, good idea! Mom has a picture of a bee from her garden that we can use to give us an idea of how to draw our picture. We can draw our flowers in any color we want.

We can't wait to see your Science Notebook. Sam and I drew lots of bees on our flowers!

Mutualism is a Symbiotic relationship where two Organisms receive a benefit

MUTUALISM IS A SYMbiotic relationship Where Two ORGANISMS receive A benefit

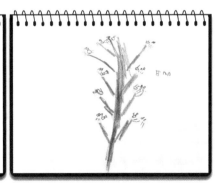

In your Science Notebook, write: **Mutualism is a symbiotic relationship where two organisms receive a benefit.**

Then, draw a picture of a bee on a flower.

Learning about parasitism this week also reminded us that we can serve others and show them God's love. Copy Philippians 2:3 on the back of your Notebook page as a reminder.

Do nothing out of selfish ambition or vain conceit. Rather, in humility value others above yourselves (Philippians 2:3).

Deciduous Biome Project

Day!

Do you know what today is? It's the day we're going to start creating our own temperate deciduous forest biome! I'm super excited to get started.

Me too! I've got a shoebox all ready to go. We'll first need to create our background, and I have an idea. Let's paint the background this time. We can paint the sky and several deciduous trees and bushes.

Activity directions:

1. Cover your table or counter with the plastic tablecloth.

2. Determine if you can paint inside your shoebox or if you will need to paint the background on paper in order for it to show. If your shoebox is dark cardboard, you may need to paint the background on paper. Be sure to cut the paper to the right size before you begin painting.

3. Begin painting your deciduous background. Some things you can paint would be the sky, deciduous trees, grass, flowers, and bushes.

4. Allow the paper or shoebox to dry. If paper was used, glue the background inside the shoebox once it is dry. Set the shoebox in a safe place — we'll add the forest floor tomorrow!

materials needed

☐ Acrylic paint

☐ Paintbrushes

☐ Shoebox or similar size box

☐ White construction paper

☐ Glue stick

☐ Tablecloth (plastic)

It's time to add the forest floor to our biome today. Do you have an idea for what we should do, Ben?

I think I've got a plan. We used paper to create the ground last time, and I think that will work this time too. Let's also go outside and see what we can gather! We may be able to find some acorns, old leaves, a twig, dirt, or grass to add to our forest floor.

Great idea. If we can find a twig, it will look like an old, fallen tree! Ready to get started?

Activity directions:

1. Cut the green construction paper to the right size so that it fits in the bottom of your shoebox.

2. Add any items you found outside to the forest floor. Ben and Hannah added a twig as a fallen tree. They also found some acorns under an old oak tree. If you can find old leaves you can tear them up for the forest floor. If you'd like, you can also draw squiggly earthworms on the forest floor.

materials needed

- [ ] Green construction paper
- [ ] Scissors
- [ ] Gather any items you can find from outside: dirt, a twig, old leaves, leaves, or acorns.

Day • • •

Let's add some deciduous trees to our biome today! We learned a lot about them in our studies. We can cut out deciduous tree shapes just like we did last time and tape them to the wooden dowels.

Okay! Let's get started on our trees. The biome will really start to look like a deciduous forest today!

Activity directions:

1. Determine how many deciduous trees you would like to create. Remember to keep some room in your biome for small plants and animals. Carefully cut tree shapes from the construction paper.

2. Ask your teacher to cut or break the wooden dowels to the height you would like your trees to be.

3. Place the dowel in the middle of the piece you cut from the construction paper and tape the dowel to the paper.

4. Form a small piece of playdough into a ball and flatten the bottom a bit. Insert the bottom of the dowel into the playdough to hold your tree upright.

5. Add the trees to the biome and put it in a safe place.

materials needed

- [ ] Green construction paper
- [ ] 1/8-inch wooden dowels (6–12 inches long)
- [ ] Tape
- [ ] Scissors
- [ ] Playdough or clay

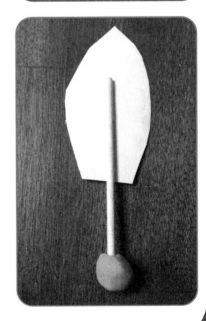

Day

Our biome is almost complete. I love the way it looks!

Me too, it sure is fun to put the biome together! Let's add some small shrubs today.

Ooh, good idea! That will create our understory and shrub layer. We can cut out some green construction paper again to make the shrubs.

Activity directions:

1. Decide how many bushes you would like to add to your biome. Cut small bush shapes from the green construction paper.

2. Fold up the bottom 1/4 inch of the bush shape as shown in the picture below. This will form a stand for your bush. You can draw fruit or flowers on your bush if you'd like.

3. Place your bush in the biome. You can also add glue to the folded stand to help hold the bush in place. Set the biome in a safe place; we'll finish it tomorrow!

materials needed

- [ ] Green construction paper
- [ ] Scissors
- [ ] Glue stick

I can't believe we're ready to finish our biome today! I have some small, model animals that we are going to put into our biome. If you don't have any, you can also use playdough to create some or ask your teacher to help you find and print some pictures you can use. Let's add our animals to the temperate deciduous forest model!

Activity directions:

1. Add the small animals to your deciduous biome model.

2. Share your biome with your family. Be sure to tell them what you've learned about the temperate deciduous forest and God's design.

materials needed

☐ Small forest animals like deer, raccoon, rabbit, fox, bear, cardinal, woodpecker, opossum, or skunk.

Bonus! Take a picture of your temperate deciduous biome and ask your teacher to help you print it out. Then, tape or glue the picture on the next page in your Science Notebook. Write **My Temperate Deciduous Biome** at the top of the page.

Color this picture of a deciduous forest.

Tropical Rainforest

Day 1

It has been so much fun exploring the boreal and temperate deciduous biomes with you! It's time to explore a new biome now. Are you ready to join us?

The next biome to explore on our adventure is the tropical rainforest. This biome is full of beauty, and even some mystery. I'm certain we'll find elements of God's amazing design here, so let's get started! Where do we find the tropical rainforest biome, Hannah?

Remember when we talked about the earth's hemispheres when we studied the boreal biome?

Yes, if we were to look at a globe and draw a pretend line around the middle of the earth, the top half would be what we call the northern hemisphere, and the bottom half would be the southern hemisphere.

Styrofoam™ ball ✓

Permanent marker ☐

Flashlight ☐

Tablecloth ☐

Dark room ☐

Right! We call the pretend line around the middle of the earth the equator. The climate near the equator is warm. Tropical rainforests grow near the equator in the southern hemisphere. Can you tell us more about the climate in the tropical rainforest, Ben?

Weekly materials list

The tropical rainforest climate is warm and rainy. I guess that is why we call it the rainforest! The tropical rainforest can receive around 80 inches of rain a year. However, some areas can receive as much as 400 inches. That is an incredible amount of rain!

When you compare that to the temperate deciduous forest, that is a lot of rain! Remember, a deciduous forest only receives about 30–60 inches of rain each year.

While the boreal and deciduous forest biomes cover much of the earth, the tropical rainforest covers just a small area of the earth. The tropical rainforest can be found in areas of Africa and India, as well as parts of Australia and Asia. The Amazon rainforest is found in Central America and is the biggest rainforest in the world.

Even though the rainforest isn't a large biome, it sounds like we'll still have a lot to explore together!

 Read each sentence below, then circle the phrase that will make the sentence true.

1. Rainforests grow near the equator in the **northern / southern** hemisphere.

2. Rainforests **do / do not** receive very much rain.

3. The climate of the rain forest is **warm and rainy / dry and hot**.

4. The rainforest is the **smallest / largest** land biome on earth.

Let's learn a little more about the tropical rainforest's climate today! One interesting thing about the rainforest climate is that this biome doesn't experience the four seasons like the deciduous or boreal forest.

We learned about how the earth's orbit around the sun causes the seasons in *Adventures in the Physical World*. Let's review the earth's orbit to learn why the rainforest doesn't have four seasons.

Great idea! Remember, the earth is a sphere and it orbits around the sun. Let's imagine there is a long pole through the center of the earth — we call this an axis. The axis helps us describe how the planet orbits and spins. The earth's axis isn't straight up and down, it is tilted to the side.

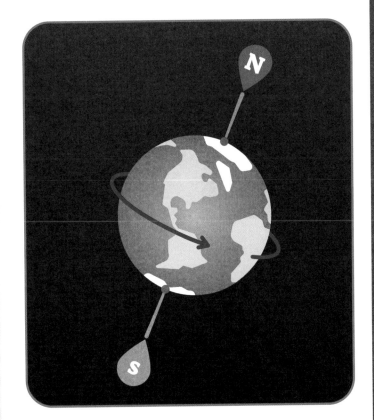

Let's talk about the equator now. As you know, the northern hemisphere is above the equator, and the southern hemisphere is below it. As the earth completes its orbit all the way around the sun, it is always tilted the same way.

On one side of the sun, the tilt of the earth means that the northern hemisphere is toward the sun. This means the northern hemisphere receives more direct light and heat from the sun — it will be summertime here! However, the southern hemisphere will be tilted away from the sun. It will receive less direct heat and light, making it winter time there.

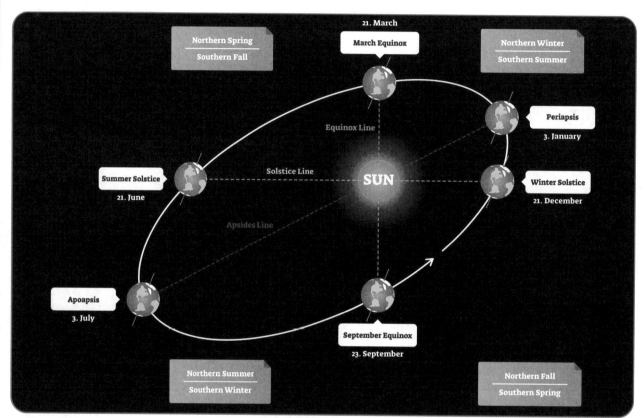

The earth will continue its orbit until it reaches the other side of the sun. On this side, the northern hemisphere is now angled away from the sun. The northern hemisphere now receives indirect light from the sun — it's winter in the northern hemisphere! The southern hemisphere is now tilted toward the sun. It is receiving direct sunlight, which makes it summer in the southern hemisphere!

But don't forget the equator! While the tilt of the earth's axis affects the light and heat the northern and southern hemispheres receive, it doesn't affect the equator as much. The equator receives about the same amount of light and heat throughout the whole year.

Activity directions:

We can use a flashlight to see direct and indirect light.

materials needed

- ☐ Flashlight
- ☐ Dark room

1. Turn out the lights in the room and turn on your flashlight.

2. Point the flashlight straight down at the ground. This creates direct light on the floor — the light is focused on one area.

3. Now, tilt the flashlight slightly. Do you see how the light spreads out over a larger area? This creates indirect light. The light isn't focused on one small area.

When light from the sun is directly on one hemisphere, it is more focused. That hemisphere will receive more light and heat, making it summertime. When the light from the sun is indirectly on one hemisphere, it is spread out over a larger area. There will be less light and heat, making it wintertime.

Bonus Activity directions:

If you'd like to see direct and indirect light in action on a model of the earth, you can complete this activity from *Adventures in the Physical World.*

*Optional: you may paint the Styrofoam™ ball to resemble planet earth and allow to dry. Be sure to spread out a tablecloth to protect the table.

1. Use the permanent marker to draw a line around the middle of the Styrofoam™ ball. This is our equator.

2. On the top half of the ball, write N for the northern hemisphere. On the bottom half, write S for the southern hemisphere.

3. Insert the skewer through the top of the northern hemisphere and push it all the way through the ball so that the ball lies on the halfway point of the skewer. This is our axis.

4. Tilt the skewer so the earth is at a slight angle.

5. Hold the flashlight 2–3 feet away from the earth, with the skewer tilted slightly toward the light. The height of the flashlight should be about even with the equator.

6. Turn on the flashlight (you may also turn off the lights in the room for a clearer view). Which hemisphere is the flashlight shining more directly on? Would it be summer or winter in that hemisphere? What about the other hemisphere?

7. Now tilt the earth toward the opposite direction. The top of the skewer should now be tilted slightly away from the light. Which hemisphere is the flashlight shining more directly on now? Would it be summer or winter in that hemisphere? What about the other hemisphere?

Day
...

I'm glad we reviewed the rotation of the earth! It helped me to understand why the tropical rainforest doesn't experience the four seasons. Are there any seasons in the tropical rainforest, though?

Actually, yes! Instead of spring, summer, fall, and winter, the tropical rainforest has a rainy season and a dry season. Sometimes these are also called the wet and dry seasons.

And as you might have guessed, the rainy season is rainy. The dry season is much drier than the rainy season, but some rain may still fall. Let's look a little closer at the Amazon rainforest. Here, the temperature tends to stay between 72° and 93° Fahrenheit all year long. The air is usually thick, hot, and humid from all the rain.

Hmm, thick and humid. Does that mean kind of like the air in the bathroom when I take a hot shower or bath and forget to turn on the exhaust fan? The air gets all hot and steamy.

That is a good example! All the moisture from the shower becomes trapped in the bathroom air, making it thick and humid. The moisture is also trapped in the rainforest air, helping to make it hot and humid too.

Ah, okay! That helps me to imagine the rainforest better. I've started reading about some of the wildlife that lives in the rainforest. The tropical rainforest is home to diverse and colorful creatures. Some of my favorite creatures that live here are toucans, poison dart frogs, hummingbirds, and chameleons. I'm excited to learn more about the animals in this biome as we explore!

We'll definitely have a lot to learn about. Let's explore the Amazon River a little more first! The Amazon River winds through much of South America. At almost 4,000 miles long, it is one of the longest rivers in the world!

 The long Amazon River is home to over 3,000 species of fish. See if you can find the names of a few of these fish in the word search below:

piranha   arapaima   jacunda   oscar   caparari

Z	X	C	V	P	I	R	A	N	H	A
M	O	W	J	A	C	U	N	D	A	B
E	S	O	R	Q	P	R	T	S	L	F
Q	C	A	P	A	R	I	E	R	K	X
C	A	P	I	N	E	C	O	N	E	R
A	R	A	P	A	I	M	A	I	B	I

piranha

jacunda

oscar

Day 8

Let's begin organizing the tropical rainforest today! Just like in the deciduous forest, we can divide the tropical rainforest into layers. In the rainforest, the very top layer is called the emergent layer.

The emergent layer holds the very tallest trees. These trees tower above the rest of the forest canopy. They can be over 200 feet tall — that's about as tall as five telephone poles all stacked on top of each other. Because they are so tall, the trees in the emergent layer receive full sunlight.

Whoa, those are really tall trees! The second layer is the canopy, just like in the deciduous forest. Trees in the canopy grow to be around 150 feet tall. That's almost as tall as four telephone poles stacked on top of each other. The upper parts of these trees receive sunlight and block out most of the light for the rest of the forest.

You might be able to guess the third layer — it's the understory! The understory contains smaller trees and shrubs. Plants in this layer can grow to be about 30 feet high, or almost as tall as a telephone pole. The final layer is the forest floor. We find some smaller plants here, as well as vines and roots.

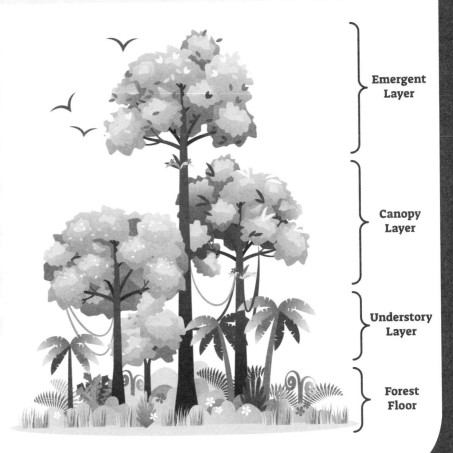

Emergent Layer

Canopy Layer

Understory Layer

Forest Floor

Each layer of the rainforest is important and provides important habitats for the creatures that live here.

I'm excited to explore the rainforest layers deeper together! Talking about all the rain in the rainforest reminded me of Psalm 147:7–9:

Sing to the LORD with grateful praise, make music to our God on the harp. He covers the sky with clouds; he supplies the earth with rain and makes grass grow on the hills. He provides food for the cattle and for the young ravens when they call.

Aren't you glad God supplies the earth with rain? I love learning about how God designed the world. There are so many different biomes we can explore, and there is always more we can be learning about God and His creation.

Day

We've started exploring a new biome, and it's time to add another page to our Science Notebook today!

Woohoo! I've got my Science Notebook here and ready to go! What should we add to it today?

Well, we talked about the rainforest climate and how rainforests are located near the equator. Let's draw a picture of the earth and add the equator.

Ooh, that sounds like fun! Here is a picture we can use as an example.

Here are our Notebook drawings; it was fun to draw the earth! I drew mine so big that I forgot to leave space for the sentence — but I still squeezed it in! You may want to write the sentence first and then draw the earth. Have fun creating!

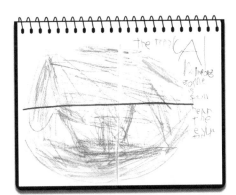

notebook

In your Science Notebook, write: **The tropical rainforest biome is found near the equator.**

Then draw a picture of the earth. Be sure to draw the equator around the middle.

Hidden Treasure

Reading about the large amount of rain the rainforest receives reminded us that God supplies the earth with rain. His design is amazing. Copy Psalm 147:8 on the back of your Notebook page as a reminder.

He covers the sky with clouds; he supplies the earth with rain and makes grass grow on the hills (Psalm 147:8).

Day

Emergent Layer

Oh good, I'm glad you're here! I'm excited to start the next part of our exploration in the tropical rainforest. What are we going to learn about next, Hannah?

Well, I thought we could take a deeper look at the emergent layer.

Don't you mean a higher look? After all, the emergent layer does tower quite high!

Oh, Ben, you're so funny. Let's look at some of the ways God designed the trees that are part of the emergent layer. These trees grow quite tall, and they need to be able to withstand the strong sunlight they receive — we'll learn more about that soon!

Okay! Let's explore the Amazon rainforest. What types of trees grow in the emergent layer there?

One of the trees we find in the emergent layer is the Brazil nut tree. This tree can reach around 160 feet high and live around 1,000 years! As you may have guessed, the Brazil nut tree produces nuts. The nuts grow inside a hard shell that looks a little like a coconut.

The hard, outer nutshell can weigh about 5 pounds. Once it is ripe, the nut falls from the tree and crashes through the forest. As it falls, it can hit a speed of almost 50 miles per hour!

You definitely wouldn't want to get hit by one of those as it falls to the ground!

No way! One animal that does love Brazil tree nuts is the agouti (said this way: ŭh-goo-tē). The agouti is a type of rodent, like a rat, squirrel, or beaver. Because the shell of the Brazil tree nut is so hard and tough, no animal is able to crack it and enjoy the nuts inside. No animal, that is, except for the agouti!

God designed the agouti with sharp teeth that can crack into the hard outer shell easily. The agouti will then eat some of the nuts, or take them and bury them to save for later. If the agouti forgets about a buried nut, it will grow into a new Brazil nut tree when the time is just right.

 God designed the agouti with strong, sharp teeth. The agouti enjoys eating Brazil tree nuts. Draw a picture of an agouti. Here is an example you can use for an idea.

Another type of tree in the emergent layer of the Amazon rainforest is the kapok (said this way: kā-pŏk) tree. The kapok tree can grow to be 200 feet tall. That is even taller than the Brazil nut tree! The kapok tree's trunk is wide; it can be 10 feet around. It makes a perfect habitat for birds, frogs, and bats.

Bats? I didn't know bats were part of the rainforest.

Bats are actually important to kapok trees. The kapok tree produces flowers that need to be pollinated.

Wait a minute! We learned about pollination in *Adventures in Creation*, but let's review it. Flowers create seeds that will later grow into a new plant or tree — but they need help to do that job. Bees, butterflies, hummingbirds, bats, and other insects help flowers. We call them **pollinators** (said this way: pŏl-ĭn-āt-ōrs).

Flowers may all look different, but they have four parts that work together. The first part is the petals. They are often brightly colored to attract pollinators to the flower. Underneath the flower you may see tiny, firm leaves. These are called sepals. Sepals help to protect the flower before it opens up.

When you look inside the flower, you may see long stems coming from the middle. These are called stamens, and they make pollen. Pollen is powdery and sticks to the legs, feathers, or fur of pollinators. The final part of the flower is called the pistil. The pistil needs to receive pollen from other flowers in order for the flower to make new seeds.

The flower creates sweet nectar for the pollinator to drink. When a pollinator lands on the flower, it also brushes up against the pollen, which sticks to its legs, feathers, or fur. When the pollinator flies to the next flower, it picks up more pollen and leaves some behind from other flowers. The flower uses the pollen to create seeds. We call this pollination, and without it, a plant or tree wouldn't be able to create new seeds.

Activity directions:

materials needed

- ☐ Craft pipe cleaner
- ☐ Flour
- ☐ Cocoa powder
- ☐ 2 plates

1. Sprinkle a little cocoa powder on one plate and flour on the second.

2. Wrap the pipe cleaner around your finger to create an insect. The ends of the pip cleaner should hang down, like legs.

3. Land your pipe cleaner insect in the flour and move it around. Then pick your finger up and examine the pipe cleaner. Do you see flour stuck to the fuzzy legs of your pipe cleaner insect?

4. Now, land your pipe cleaner insect in the cocoa powder and move it around. Then pick up your finger and examine the pipe cleaner. Do you see flour and cocoa powder stuck to it? Look at the plate. Is there flour on the cocoa plate now?

It's time to get back to our exploration today! We were talking about the kapok tree yesterday, but we paused to learn about pollination quickly. It's time to get right back to bats and the kapok tree now!

I love smelling different flowers. I would imagine the flowers from such a tall tree would smell so good!

Actually, not all flowers have a good scent. The kapok tree's blossoms don't smell very good. Their stinky scent attracts bats to the flowers to pollinate them. The bats enjoy the flower's nectar as pollen covers their fur.

Then when the bat flies over to the next flower, it leaves some pollen behind and picks up pollen from the new flower. And it thinks it is only enjoying a good meal!

Exactly! The bat enjoys a good meal, and the kapok tree is pollinated so that more seeds can be produced. This is another relationship God put in place in creation.

The bats and the kapok trees have a symbiotic relationship. They both receive a benefit. This is a relationship of mutualism.

Way to remember those relationships, Ben! The kapok tree's seeds develop inside fruit that looks a bit like a bean pod. When the fruit opens, the seeds look like silky cotton. The silky seeds can be picked up by the wind and be carried quite far across the rainforest. In time, these seeds may grow into new kapok trees.

 applyit Bats help pollinate kapok trees. Help the bat through the maze to the kapok tree.

 You can read more about bats and hummingbirds in *God's Big Book of Animals*.

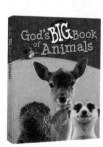

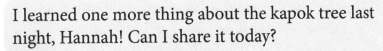

Day I learned one more thing about the kapok tree last night, Hannah! Can I share it today?

Absolutely! What are you waiting for?

The kapok tree has a special kind of root that helps to keep the tall tree stable. The bottom of the trunk fans out in wide, triangle shapes. These are called **buttress roots** (said this way: bŭh-trĭs). Buttress roots give the tree a stable foundation and also help to draw nutrients into the tree.

A stable foundation is really important, especially for a tree that grows as tall as the kapok tree!

The buttress roots remind me of how the Bible also talks about God as our firm foundation. God's word and His truth is the only firm foundation we can build our lives on — it is the only thing that will never change.

That is a good reminder, Ben. It makes me think of Hannah's prayer in the Bible in 1 Samuel 2. Hannah had prayed for a long time for God to give her a son. God answered her prayer and Samuel was born. In verse 2, Hannah said:

There is no one holy like the LORD; there is no one besides you; there is no Rock like our God (1 Samuel 2:2).

In her prayer, Hannah also talks about the Lord's sovereignty (said this way: sŏv-rĭn-tē). Sovereignty is a big word that means God has power and authority over all things. Sometimes, things around me can feel crazy or out of control. But Mom and Dad remind me that God is sovereign. He is in control, and He is our firm foundation.

We're going to add a new page to our Science Notebook today!

Yay! This is always my favorite day. I love getting to document what we've learned about like a real scientist. We talked about the emergent layer, and also about pollinators and bats. It was neat to learn how bats help the kapok tree.

I agree. Let's add a bat to our Science Notebook this week. Here is a sketch we can use for an example.

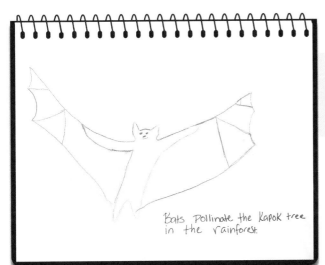

Bats Pollinate the Kapok tree in the rainforest.

Here is what we drew in our Notebooks! I think Ben drew the happiest bat I've ever seen.

BATS Pollinate the kapok in the rainforest

Oh thanks, Hannah! I love Sam's colorful bat. It looks really happy too. I hope you have as much fun drawing as we did!

In your Science Notebook, write: **Bats pollinate the kapok tree in the rainforest.**

Then, draw a picture of a bat.

Learning about the buttress roots of the kapok tree this week also reminded us that a firm foundation is very important. God is the only firm foundation we can build our lives upon. Copy 1 Samuel 2:2 on the back of your Notebook page as a reminder.

There is no one holy like the LORD; there is no one besides you; there is no Rock like our God (1 Samuel 2:2).

Canopy

Day 1

Now that we've explored the emergent layer, it's time to learn more about the next layer of the tropical rainforest! Do you remember what the second layer of the rainforest is? It's the forest canopy! Just like in the deciduous forest, the canopy is a dense layer of trees that form an umbrella over the rest of the rainforest.

In the tropical rainforest, the canopy can reach about 100 feet tall. The trees, leaves, and plants that grow in the canopy form a very dense covering over the rainforest. Dense is a word that means very thick.

Since the canopy is so dense, then I guess it is mostly just the trees and plants that live in this layer?

Actually, the rainforest canopy is home to most of the creatures that live in the rainforest! We'll learn about a few of those creatures later on. In the meantime, the canopy is an incredibly interesting place to explore.

In the tropical rainforest, the upper part of the canopy receives the most sunlight. The leaves that grow near the top of the canopy are often coated in a waxy layer — just like coniferous needles.

Ooh, the waxy layer means water cannot evaporate as quickly from the leaf. This protects water inside the tree's leaves from the heat of the sun.

Exactly! Just like in the deciduous forest, the upper canopy absorbs most of the sunlight —but a little sunlight still filters through to the lower canopy. Leaves that are lower on the tree are often darker colors than the leaves on the upper part. This helps the lower leaves absorb more of the small amount of sunlight that filters through.

Wow, God thought of everything!

I thought that was a neat design too! We have to go finish our chores now, but we'll explore more of the plants that grow in the canopy tomorrow. See you soon, friend!

---

applyit Fill in the missing word for each sentence.

darker   upper   100   evaporating   dense

1. The rainforest canopy can reach about _____ feet tall.

2. The _____ canopy absorbs most of the sunlight.

3. Leaves that grow lower in the canopy are often _____ .

4. The waxy layer on leaves keeps water from _____ .

5. The rainforest canopy is very _____ .

I've been reading about some of the plants that grow in the rainforest canopy. I'm excited to share what I've learned with you today!

Oh good, I always love to hear about what you've been learning. What can you tell us about plants in the canopy, Ben?

Well, the rainforest canopy is home to a special type of plant called **epiphyte** (said this way: ĕp-ŭh-fīte). Epiphytes are a type of plant that grow on top of other plants.

Hmm, if they grow on top of other plants, do they also take nutrients away from the other plant? Are they like parasites?

No, epiphytes don't take nutrients from the plant they're growing on. Epiphytes only use the other plant for support. This allows the epiphyte plant to grow high up in the canopy where it can also receive the sunlight it needs.

Oh! Sunlight is important for many rainforest plants — but the forest floor in this biome is quite dark. These plants would have a difficult time growing on the forest floor! I'm curious, though — how are they able to grow on other plants without soil and without taking nutrients from the other plant?

Good question! The cracks and grooves of tree limbs and trunks catch falling leaf material from the canopy. As this material decays, it gives epiphytes nutrients, just like soil does. Some epiphytes are also able to absorb water and nutrients from the air around them!

What is most interesting about these plants, though, is the relationships they have with other creatures that live in the canopy. I have to go help Mom get lunch ready now, but we'll talk more about those relationships tomorrow!

 Orchids are one type of beautiful epiphyte plant. Draw orchids on a tree below. Here is an example of some growing on a tree.

I've been wondering about the relationships between epiphytes and other creatures in the canopy since yesterday. I can't wait to get started!

Well, then what are we waiting for? Let's dive right in. Some types of epiphyte plants have a special shape that collects water — like a cup or a bucket would. Their leaves spread out and catch falling rain, which puddles in the middle of the plant.

Neat! The water doesn't just drain out right away?

No. Plants like the tank bromeliad (said this way: brō-mē-lē-ăd) will hold on to the water collected by the leaves. This stored water creates a tiny pond way up in the canopy — and it is very important. The canopy is the home of most rainforest animals. These animals also need water to drink, and epiphyte plants work like a bucket to collect water that creatures can drink.

Wow! God's design even cares for the animals that live so high up in the canopy!

But it doesn't end there! Epiphytes also provide a habitat to the **amphibians** (said this way: ăm-fíb-ē-ĕns) that live high in the canopy. Amphibians are animals like frogs, toads, and salamanders. One type of amphibian that lives in the tropical rainforest is the brightly colored poison dart frog!

Poison dart frogs lay eggs. Once the eggs hatch, the baby frogs are called tadpoles. The adult frog will carry the tadpoles to an epiphyte, like the tank bromeliad, where they can swim and grow. But that still isn't the end!

The amphibians, insects, and other creatures that live in or visit the epiphyte plant leave waste behind. Remember, waste is another word for poop. The waste collects in the epiphyte along with the water. This waste has nutrients available in it, just like earthworm waste does. Some plants are able to absorb nutrients from the waste in the water! This is important since the plants can't always receive nutrients through their roots.

Wow! I've noticed that nothing gets wasted in creation; it gets recycled and used for other things. I think that is really amazing!

applyit

Bright colors often warn predators that their prey is poisonous. Poison dart frogs are poisonous if a predator tries to eat them. Though their bright colors are a warning, the colors and patterns on a poison dart frog are also beautiful! Color the poison dart frog below with bright colors.

Hasn't the rainforest canopy been interesting to explore? I especially enjoyed hearing about the relationship between the tank bromeliad and the poison dart frog.

It was fun to read about that! I'm also excited to learn more about other creatures that live in the canopy later on.

I've been thinking about the poison dart frog today. It is so bright and beautiful — but also poisonous. It can harm or even kill another creature. It reminds me of James 3:7–10:

All kinds of animals, birds, reptiles and sea creatures are being tamed and have been tamed by mankind, but no human being can tame the tongue. It is a restless evil, full of deadly poison. With the tongue we praise our Lord and Father, and with it we curse human beings, who have been made in God's likeness. Out of the same mouth come praise and cursing. My brothers and sisters, this should not be.

The word *curse* can mean saying a bad word or saying unkind words to hurt someone else. Have you ever said something mean in order to hurt someone else? I know I have when I've been angry at Ben. I've said hurtful things that I've apologized for later. Our tongues are important because we can use them to encourage and help someone else, or to hurt them deeply. When we use our tongues to hurt others, it's like they are full of poison.

Just like the poison dart frog, we can make ourselves look really good on the outside. But if we use our tongues to hurt others, it's like we are full of poison.

That is a really good reminder, Hannah. I want to use my tongue to help others and to speak kind words to them.

Me too. Sometimes it is hard to speak kind words when we are angry. But we can pray and ask God to help us guard our tongues so that we do not say unkind things. Let's talk with Dad and Mom tonight about ways we can guard our tongues. I'm sure they have ideas that can help us too!

You can learn more about the poison dart frog in *God's Big Book of Animals*.

Well, here we are! It's time to add a new page to our Science Notebook. I've got mine all ready to go. Did you bring yours, friend?

I've got mine too! Let's draw an epiphyte today. What do you think?

I like that! I have a picture we can use to give us an idea for what to draw, here it is!

Here is what we drew in our Notebooks. I added some birds to my picture. Have fun creating yours!

In your Science Notebook, write: **An epiphyte is a plant that grows on another plant or tree.**

Then draw a picture of an epiphyte on a tree.

Learning about the poison dart frog this week also reminded us that unkind words can be like poison to others. Copy James 7:10 on the back of your Notebook page as a reminder.

Out of the same mouth come praise and cursing. My brothers and sisters, this should not be (James 7:10).

Birds of the Canopy

Day

We're here and ready for another adventure! What are we going to explore, Hannah?

Well, I hope you don't mind staying in the canopy for a little while longer! I thought it would be fun to explore the wildlife that lives there. Along the way we'll discover some of the ways God designed these rainforest creatures.

Ooh, that sounds like fun since most rainforest creatures live in the canopy!

We can start by learning about some birds that live in this layer of the rainforest.

When we talk about animals or birds, we often talk about their kind. A **kind** is a family group of animals. For example, there is the bear kind. There are many different types of bears like black bears, polar bears, and brown bears. However, each type of bear is part of the bear kind.

So, another example would be the cat kind. Our pet cat is named Bell, and she's just a little black cat. But tigers and lions are also part of the cat kind. Lions, tigers, and pet cats are each different, but all part of the same cat kind that God created on the sixth day of creation.

God created many different types of birds, and we can organize birds into groups like sparrows, pigeons, and parrots. Parrots are birds that live in tropical environments. God created parrots with feet that have a special design for climbing tall trees. Parrots have four toes on their feet. Two toes point forward, and two point backward. Parrots use their feet and beak to quickly climb any tree.

There are many types of parrots, but my favorite type is called the macaw (said this way: mŭh-kåw). There are 17 different types of macaws, but two of my favorite types can be found in the Amazon rainforest: the scarlet macaw and the blue and gold macaw. The scarlet macaw's feathers are bright red, blue, and yellow. The blue and gold macaw's feathers are bright blue and yellow. We'll learn a little more about these birds tomorrow!

Look at the pictures below and write **scarlet macaw** or **blue and gold macaw** to label each.

 Scarlet is a word that means red. Since the scarlet macaw is mostly red, that will help you remember its name.

Day

I'm excited to learn more about those beautiful macaws today, Hannah! Remember when we went to the zoo last summer? We stopped to watch the macaws for a bit. They were fun to watch.

They were! Let's learn a little more about them. The scarlet macaw and the blue and gold macaw live in the rainforests of Central America. Both of these types of macaws can be almost 3 feet tall and weigh a little over 2 pounds. Other types of macaws can be a little bigger than that, though!

Macaws prefer to live in a pair of two or in family groups, so you won't usually find one all alone. Macaws are very loyal and can live for a long time in the wild. Blue and gold macaws can live for 25 years, while scarlet macaws can live to be around 50 years old!

Wow! I'm curious, what do macaws eat?

Macaws are herbivores — that means they eat plants. Macaws like to eat berries and seeds. Their beak is also strong enough to break through some types of tough nutshells. Macaws can use their four-toed feet like a hand to hold on to the nut while they use their beak to crush and pry open the shell.

Interesting! I have one other question; don't their bright colors make them stand out to predators in the rainforest?

Actually, those bright colors are perfectly suited for the tropical rainforest. Macaws can blend in with brightly colored fruits and flowers, as well as the shadows of the rainforest. When they are together in a group, their bright colors distract and confuse predators.

Macaws also find safe, hidden-away places for their nests. Macaws do not build nests like other birds. Instead, they find holes within trees. Macaws lay their eggs in the tree hole where the eggs will be safe from predators.

Thanks for telling us about macaws, Hannah! These beautiful parrots remind me of God's creativity and wisdom in their design. I can't wait to go back to the zoo and watch them again!

Macaws are big, beautiful parrots. Color the macaw with bright colors.

 Macaws can be quite noisy, and some can even learn to mimic human words. Ask your teacher to help you find a video of noisy macaws. Can you mimic the noises they make?

There are many types of parrots and birds that live in the rainforest. I wish we had time to explore them all! I think the harpy eagle (said this way: härpē ē-gŭhl) is especially interesting, though, because it is the biggest and strongest bird in the rainforest. The harpy eagle isn't a parrot, it is a raptor. **Raptors** (said this way: răp-ters) are predator birds.

The harpy eagle is a carnivore then?

Yes. The harpy eagle is a carnivore — it eats meat. It mostly eats sloths and monkeys, though sometimes it may hunt other birds like macaws. I was sad to read that. But, it's a reminder of how sin has affected creation and broken God's original design.

It sure is. Tell us more about the harpy eagle. What makes it unique?

Well, macaws are brightly colored, but the harpy eagle is quite plain. It is mostly grey and white, with an oddly shaped crown of feathers on the back of its head. These feathers work a little like a speaker for the harpy eagle. When the feathers are raised, they direct sound right into the harpy eagle's ears so it can hear even better.

The harpy eagle has thick, strong legs and a sharp curved beak. It has claws — we call them talons (said this way: tăl-ŭhns) on birds — that can be 5 inches long!

The harpy eagle is an impressive hunter, but it's important to remember that God originally designed it to eat plants. I imagine the beak and talons would be great for eating fruits and vegetables too!

The harpy eagle is a skilled predator. Color the harpy eagle and review the features that make it a unique, strong predator in the rainforest.

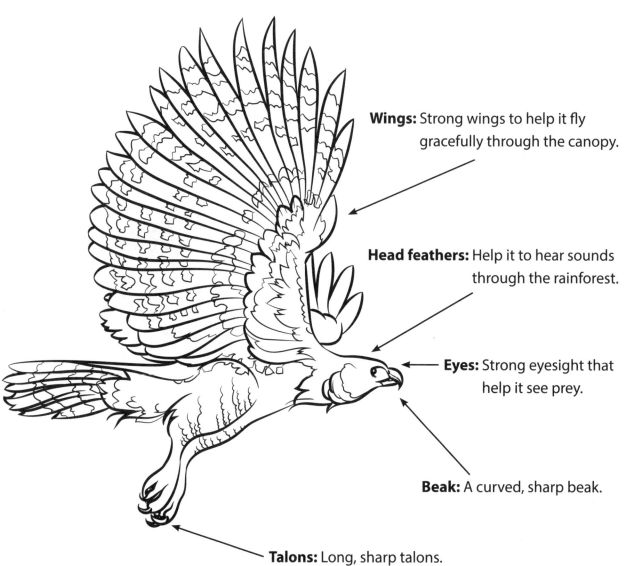

Wings: Strong wings to help it fly gracefully through the canopy.

Head feathers: Help it to hear sounds through the rainforest.

Eyes: Strong eyesight that help it see prey.

Beak: A curved, sharp beak.

Talons: Long, sharp talons.

Toucans also live in the rainforest canopy. You can learn more about toucans in *God's Big Book of Animals*.

Day

It was fun learning about macaws and the harpy eagle this week!

I thought so too! I want to learn more about rainforest birds after school today. I'll have to do some more reading for sure.

I love looking at the bright colors and patterns many types of parrots have in the rainforest. God created so many different kinds of birds with a great variety of colors and patterns.

Some birds are plain, like the common sparrow, while others are so brightly colored. God created each one uniquely with the design it would need to survive. The common sparrow and the bright parrots both display the glory and care of God. I've been thinking about Matthew 10:29–31 this week. Let's read it together:

Are not two sparrows sold for a penny? Yet not one of them will fall to the ground outside your Father's care. And even the very hairs of your head are all numbered. So don't be afraid; you are worth more than many sparrows.

Right before this passage, Jesus was reminding His followers to not be afraid and that God would care for them no matter what happened. God cares for even the common sparrow, and He cares for you too. Whether you see the bright feathers of the macaw or the brown pattern of the common sparrow, remember that God is caring for that bird, and He is caring much more for you.

Let's add another page to our Science Notebook today!

You don't have to ask me twice. This is my favorite day! I'd love to draw a scarlet macaw in our Notebook today. I found this picture that we can use for an idea!

Ooh, I like that one! There are a lot of details to draw on the macaw — but we can do it! Remember, your drawing doesn't have to look exactly the same as the picture of the macaw. Each of our drawings are always different, and they show the creativity God has given us.

Sometimes it helps to look at the shape of the object we're drawing. We can start with a long oval for our bird, and then add in the details like the beak, eyes, and wings. This is going to be fun!

I think so too. Once the scarlet macaw is drawn, we can use this picture to help us color it in.

Here is what our Notebooks look like! We hope you have as much fun drawing the scarlet macaw as we did.

notebook

In your Science Notebook, write: **The scarlet macaw lives in the rainforest.**

Then, draw a picture of a scarlet macaw and color it.

Hidden Treasure

Learning about parrots this week also reminded us that God cares for even the birds. We don't have to be afraid because God cares much more for us. Copy Matthew 10:31 on the back of your Notebook page as a reminder.

So don't be afraid; you are worth more than many sparrows (Matthew 10:31).

The Sloth

Day

I hope you've been enjoying our learning adventure as we've explored the rainforest canopy!

Are you ready to learn about one unique creature that lives in the canopy? I've been reading about the three-toed sloth lately — and it is so interesting!

Oh, I remember seeing a sloth at the zoo this summer! It had kind of a silly looking grin on its face. But the sloth just stayed hanging on the same place of the tree. It never moved the whole time we were there! It seemed rather boring. Are you sure this is an interesting creature, Hannah?

I'm sure! The sloth may be known as a slow, lazy creature, but if we stop for a moment to learn about it, we'll also find God's design. First, though, it's time to organize!

We can organize animals into groups, just like we saw with birds. The sloth is organized as a mammal. A **mammal** (said this way: măm-ŭhl) is a type of creature that has a body with hair, has a spine, and their babies drink milk.

What is a spine?

A spine is the long column of bones in your back. Your spine allows you to move and bend.

Wait, does that make me a mammal too?

Yes. Remember, science helps us to organize and talk about the things we are learning about. Scientists organize humans as mammals. This helps them to talk about and study mankind's design. We do see some similar designs between animals and people. For example, you, a bear, a sloth, and a dog all have a spine.

That points to God being the designer of each! If you look at my Science Notebook, you'll see the same handwriting in each drawing. Some of the pictures even look similar. That is because I designed each of them.

Right! We know from the Bible that God created all things, including animals and people. Though we may see some similarities in design, we also know that God created men and women different from the animals. God only gave people the ability to have a relationship with Him.

applyit God created people and animals to be different. Can you think of any ways you are different from an animal? What is something you can do that an animal cannot do? Write your answer below.

Day

The three-toed sloth is often found in the Amazon rainforest. Its name comes from the three hooked claws on its hands and feet. A sloth's claws are long and strong. The sloth uses its claws to wrap around a tree limb, and it can hang from the limb all day and all night.

Sloths are known as the world's slowest mammal because they do not move around very much. When a sloth does move, it moves very slowly.

What makes them so slow?

A sloth is an herbivore that eats leaves from the rainforest trees. These leaves are tough for the sloth's stomach to digest. The sloth's stomach has a special design that allows it to digest the tough leaves, but it can still take a week or much longer for just one meal to be digested!

Digestion (said this way: dī-jĕs-chĕn) is the process our bodies use to break down the food we eat into nutrients we can absorb and energy we can use.

The leaves that the sloth eats also do not contain very much energy for the sloth to use. So, the sloth travels very slowly and sleeps most of the day. This allows it to use very little energy compared to other animals.

So we would call them slow, but sloths actually use the energy they have available very efficiently. **Efficiently** (said this way: ĭh-fĭsh-ŭhnt-lē) means in the best way, without wasting anything.

Exactly! Though the sloth is strong enough to hang on tree limbs all day, its legs are not strong enough for it to walk on. When it is on the ground, the sloth can only crawl.

Once each week, a three-toed sloth will slowly climb down the tree so that it can, well, poop on the forest floor. Since they must crawl and move slowly, it is dangerous for the sloth to be on the forest floor. A predator could find them! Most other creatures in the canopy poop up in the trees, so scientists wondered why sloths make such a dangerous journey to the forest floor. Tomorrow we will learn a little about why they may do it.

Imagine you are a sloth, with very little energy to use. How can you use your energy efficiently? Ask your teacher to give you a job to do, then set a timer for 5 minutes. Try to complete the job before the timer rings, but you must do it very slowly the way a sloth might.

A sloth may only travel around 123 feet each day. If you have a measuring tape and the space, ask your teacher to help you measure out 15 feet. Mark the beginning and end. Then, see how quickly you can walk that distance eight times — this will be about how far a sloth moves in a day. Can you imagine taking all day long to travel that far?

I'm curious what we'll learn about today since we ended yesterday talking about sloth poop. It sounds like today's adventure could be gross!

Remember what we learned when we studied epiphytes? Even insect and animal waste can have a purpose in an environment. Sometimes scientists study the sticky, dirty, stinky, and yucky parts of creation to learn more about how things work on the earth.

Let's look at a sloth's fur first. Do you notice that the fur has a bit of a green color?

Because the sloth moves so slowly, algae is able to grow on its fur. The algae gives a sloth's fur a green color. This helps the sloth stay camouflaged in the forest canopy.

Camouflage (said this way: kǎ-mǔh-flåzh) means a way to stay hidden in an environment.

Sloths and algae have a symbiotic relationship. The sloth's fur gives algae a structure to grow on, and the algae's color helps the sloth stay hidden from predators in the canopy.

That's mutualism — both receive a benefit! But that isn't the only thing that lives in a sloth's fur. Sloth fur helps to create a whole ecosystem where beetles, insects, and moths can all live. One type of moth can only be found living in the fur of a sloth — and they help the sloth too.

Wait, a moth can help a sloth?

Yes! The moth helps the sloth's fur to stay full of nutrients the algae needs to grow. Healthier algae means better camouflage for the sloth. But the moths need a place to lay their eggs and their favorite place is — sloth poop.

Ew!

Remember, waste is another word for animal poop. Each week when a sloth travels down the tree, moths will lay their eggs in the sloth's waste. When the eggs hatch, the baby moths — or **larva** (said this way: lăr-vŭh) — will eat the waste because there are nutrients in it for them. When the sloth comes back down the tree, the new adult moths will then move into its fur and help algae grow.

Wow, the sloth, algae, and moths are all depending on each other! You were right, Hannah, the sloth is definitely an interesting creature. I'm glad scientists ask questions and even study the gross parts of creation so that we can learn more about the sloth's symbiotic relationships.

Color this picture of a sloth. Don't forget to add some green to its fur!

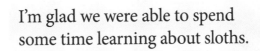

I'm glad we were able to spend some time learning about sloths.

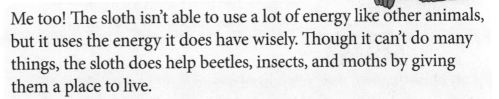

Me too! The sloth isn't able to use a lot of energy like other animals, but it uses the energy it does have wisely. Though it can't do many things, the sloth does help beetles, insects, and moths by giving them a place to live.

I've been thinking about how God gives each of us different talents, skills, and abilities to use wisely. I love doing math, for example. You're really good at helping people, Hannah.

Thanks, Ben! I'm not as good at math as you are, but I can still do my very best. We don't all have the same talents and abilities — but we can always do our very best and use what God has given us wisely.

That reminds me of Colossians 3:23–24:

Whatever you do, work at it with all your heart, as working for the Lord, not for human masters, since you know that you will receive an inheritance from the Lord as a reward. It is the Lord Christ you are serving.

This week, the sloth reminded me that whether I have a little or a lot, I can still do my very best. Whether I'm doing my schoolwork or my chores, I can work as if I'm doing it for Jesus.

Thanks for sharing with us, Ben! Sometimes I do my very best and things still don't turn out the way I want them to. That can be frustrating! But when it happens, I try to remember that I can keep on doing my very best, ask Jesus to help me, and work to keep learning. Let's ask Mom and Dad how we can use our talents wisely later today!

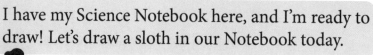

I have my Science Notebook here, and I'm ready to draw! Let's draw a sloth in our Notebook today.

That sounds like fun! I found this picture that we can use for an idea.

Oh, I like that one. Doesn't it have a cute face? Once we've drawn our sloth, we can also color it in — don't forget to add some green algae to its fur.

Here is what we drew in our Notebooks! Sam drew two sloths, and even a parrot flying through the sky. It was helpful for us to start by drawing the branch first, then draw the sloth underneath the branch. Have fun creating your sloth!

notebook

In your Science Notebook, write: **The three-toed sloth uses its energy efficiently.**

Then, draw a picture of a sloth.

Learning about how the sloth uses its energy wisely this week also reminded us that we can use our talents and abilities wisely too. We serve Jesus in all that we do, and we can always do our very best. Copy Colossians 3:23 on the back of your Notebook page as a reminder.

Whatever you do, work at it with all your heart, as working for the Lord, not for human masters (Colossians 3:23).

Monkeys of the Canopy

Day

Welcome back, friend! We've been exploring the canopy in the tropical rainforest lately, and I hope you've had as much fun as we have!

We're almost ready to begin exploring the rainforest's understory. But first, let's learn about one other kind of animal that lives in the canopy: monkeys! Several species of monkeys live in the Amazon rainforest. I've been reading about two of those species: the spider monkey and howler monkey. Let's learn about them together!

spider monkey   **howler monkey**

Ooh, this is going to be a lot of fun! Let's start with the howler monkey. I'm guessing from its name that this is a noisy species of monkey?

You're exactly right! The howler monkey gets its name from the loud call it is able to make. Howler monkeys have a bone in their throat called the hyoid bone (said this way: hī-ōy-d).

People have a hyoid bone too; it's located in our necks. This special bone helps us to be able to swallow and speak.

God designed the howler monkey with a very large hyoid bone. It acts like a megaphone or a speaker so that the howler monkey can howl across a long distance. In some cases, a howler monkey's call can be heard almost 3 miles away!

Wow! Does their howl sound like the howl of a wolf then?

No, the noise a howler monkey makes is very different from a wolf. The howler monkey's call sounds more like a growl, roar, or even a really long burp. They use their calls to let other howler monkeys know they are there and to warn others of danger. Howler monkeys are the loudest and biggest monkey in the Amazon rainforest. We'll learn more about their design tomorrow because right now, I want you to hear their loud call!

applyit Ask your teacher to help you find a video of a howler monkey howling. How would you describe the noise to a friend? Write your answer below.

Day

Howler monkeys sure are loud! Their call didn't sound like I expected it to — it's definitely an interesting noise. I'm excited to learn more today. What else can you tell us about the howler monkey, Ben?

Hmm, let's learn two new words so that we can talk more about howler monkeys. The first word is male. **Male** (said this way: māl) is another word for a boy or man. **Female** (said this way: fē-māl) is another word for a girl or woman. Just like people, animals can be boys or girls, and we use these words to describe them.

Howler monkeys are mammals. The male howler monkey can grow to be around 25 inches tall — and their tail can be just as long as their body! Males can weigh around 30 pounds, and they are bigger than the females. Female howler monkeys can grow to be around 20 inches tall and weigh about 16 pounds.

There are different types of howler monkeys, but one interesting type is the black howler monkey. Black howler monkey babies are born with brown-colored fur. As they grow, however, the male black howler monkey's fur will turn black. The female's fur will stay the same brown color for her whole life.

Neat! What do howler monkeys eat?

They eat mostly leaves and fruit. Like the sloth, they don't receive a lot of energy from their food. Howler monkeys must use their energy efficiently, so they usually spend much of the day resting or sleeping.

The howler monkey lives its life in the trees of the canopy. It climbs and balances on tree limbs or vines, which can be difficult and even dangerous! God designed the howler monkey with a **prehensile tail** (said this way: prē-hĕn-sīl). A prehensile tail can be used to hold on to things and support the monkey. We'll learn more about prehensile tails tomorrow!

apply it Write the missing word in each sentence:

bigger   prehensile   canopy   mammals

1. Howler monkeys are _____ .

2. The male howler monkey is _____ than the female howler monkey.

3. Howler monkeys live in the _____ .

4. A _____ tail can be used to hold on to things and support a monkey.

Use a measuring tape to measure out 25 inches. This is how tall a male howler monkey can be — and their tales can be that long as well! Now, measure 20 inches. This is how tall a female howler monkey can be.

Another common type of monkey in the Amazon rainforest is the spider monkey. Spider monkeys also have a prehensile tail, just like the howler monkey. Spider and howler monkeys use their tails to hold on to something (like a branch), to swing from, or to hold their weight from. A prehensile tail can be used almost like another hand — just without any fingers.

The tail of the spider and howler monkey is covered with fur, except for the bottom end. Instead, the bottom has tough skin that can firmly grip tree branches and vines. This is important because the monkeys use their tail just like a safety rope.

Have you ever watched someone climb a mountain or move through a zip-line course? They use strong clips, hooks, and ropes to protect themselves. If the person were to slip, the rope would catch them so that they don't fall. Spider and howler monkeys use their tails in a very similar way. As the monkeys move through the canopy, they wrap their tails around other branches and vines. If they were to slip, their tail would hold on to the branch and catch them.

Ah, and if the bottom of the tail was all furry, it wouldn't be able to keep such a strong grip.

Right! Spider monkeys have long, strong limbs that they use to swing, climb, and leap through the forest canopy. They are graceful and fast as they travel through the rainforest!

Spider monkeys eat mostly fruits and nuts, though they can also eat leaves, insects, and eggs. Their diet, or what they eat, is important to the tropical rainforest because fruit and nuts contain seeds.

After a spider monkey picks some fruit, it will eat the fruit or drop it in another part of the forest. The seeds the monkey eats will pass through their stomach and be left in the monkey's waste. Seeds that have been dropped from the fruit or left in waste will be able to grow later on. The spider monkey helps seeds travel, or disperse, throughout the rainforest so that new plants and trees can grow.

Tell your teacher how spider monkeys help seeds disperse through the forest.

Ask your teacher to help you find a video of a spider monkey swinging through the rainforest. Watch how they use their tails to swing and grip.

I enjoyed learning about howler and spider monkeys this week. What a neat design God gave the monkey's tail — it's perfect for their life high in the canopy. I also think it's interesting how an animal, like the spider monkey, can help seeds disperse through an environment.

I can't wait to get back to the zoo this summer and watch the spider monkeys play.

I've been thinking about protection as we've been learning over the last few days. We talked about how the monkey's tail helps to keep it safe. We also talked about how people use special ropes, hooks, and clips to protect them when they climb.

The spider monkey swings through the rainforest at a dangerous height, but it doesn't worry because it trusts its tail to keep it safe. In the same way, no matter what we walk through in life, we don't have to worry because we can trust that God is in control.

That reminds me of what king David wrote in Psalm 5:11–12,

But let all who take refuge in you be glad; let them ever sing for joy. Spread your protection over them, that those who love your name may rejoice in you. Surely, LORD, you bless the righteous; you surround them with your favor as with a shield.

Do you remember when we talked about God as our refuge in our very first science adventure this year? It means that we choose to build our lives in God and to trust in Him. David went through many difficult, dangerous, and even scary things in his life. But he learned to trust God no matter what was happening around him.

Our world is imperfect because of sin. But God is always trustworthy, faithful, and working things out to show His glory in our lives — and that is a good reason to rejoice.

I'm just about ready to learn about the understory layer of the rainforest — but first, it's Science Notebook day! I've got my Notebook and some watercolor pencils all ready to go.

I sure do enjoy adding a new page to my Science Notebook. It's really starting to fill up now! What should we draw today?

Let's draw a howler monkey! I have a picture here that we can use for an example.

We had a lot of fun drawing our howler monkeys. Here's what they look like!

notebook

In your Science Notebook, write: **The howler monkey has a prehensile tail.**

Then, draw a picture of a howler monkey.

Learning about spider and howler monkeys this week reminded us that God is always trustworthy, faithful, and working things out to show His glory in our lives. Copy Psalm 5:11a on the back of your Notebook page as a reminder.

But let all who take refuge in you be glad; let them ever sing for joy (Psalm 5:11a).

The Understory

Day

I've had so much fun learning about the rainforest's canopy over the last few weeks with you. We could spend a very long time exploring all the birds, plants, and animals that live there! But we have more to learn about in the rest of the rainforest.

We sure do! Now it's time to travel down to the next layer of the rainforest, the understory. Just like in the deciduous forest, the understory is found underneath the rainforest canopy. Very little sunlight reaches the understory because the canopy blocks most of it. We find small, young trees growing in the understory. Plants that only need a little sunlight also grow in this layer.

One interesting thing about the plants that grow in the understory is that the leaves are often larger and wider than the leaves we find in other places of the rainforest. Can you think of a reason that might be, Ben?

Hmm, let's see. . . . There isn't a lot of sunlight available for plants in the understory. Do bigger leaves allow the plants to absorb more of the sunlight that is available?

Yes, bigger leaves allow the plant to absorb all the sunlight that it can. This means the plant can still photosynthesize, even without a lot of sunlight available.

We also find many vines in the understory. Vines begin growing on the forest floor, but they don't have a strong structure. Instead, they use other trees to provide structure. The vine will attach, or wrap itself, around a tree. Then, it will grow taller in order to reach sunlight higher in the rainforest. Once the vine reaches sunlight, it may also spread outward to other trees, which creates a pathway that creatures can travel across.

The plants in the rainforest can create such a thick covering that there are places even scientists haven't been able to explore! But that doesn't stop animals, amphibians, reptiles, and insects from creating their home in this rich environment. We find many creatures living in this layer, just like in the canopy. We'll explore more soon!

---

 applyit Read each sentence below, then circle the phrase that will make the sentence true.

1. A plant's leaves are often **small / large** in the understory.

2. **Very little / lots of** sunlight reaches the understory.

3. Vines **need / do not need** a strong structure to grow on.

4. Small, young **flowers / trees** grow in the understory.

I'm excited to get started today! I've been learning about a creature that is often found in the understory. First, though, we need to learn a new word! A **reptile** (said this way: rĕp-tīl) is an animal that crawls on its belly or has small legs. Reptiles are also cold-blooded. This means their bodies rely on the sun and the air around them to keep them warm.

People and most animals are warm-blooded. That means that our bodies usually keep themselves at a consistent temperature, even if the air around us is hot or cold.

We organize snakes, lizards, turtles, and even crocodiles as reptiles. The boa constrictor (said this way: bō-ŭh kŭn-strĭk-ter) is part of the snake kind. Boa constrictors can grow to be between 6 and 10 feet long. These snakes are carnivores that travel throughout the rainforest. They eat small animals like lizards, bats, or mice. As the boa constrictor grows, it can eat bigger animals as well.

Some snakes, like rattlesnakes, are **venomous** (said this way: vĕn-ŭh-mŭhs). Venom is a special type of poison some creatures can inject through a bite or a sting. For example, bees and wasps inject venom when they sting someone. The venom is part of the reason why the sting hurts so much!

The boa constrictor is non-venomous. This means that it does not have venom. Instead, a boa constrictor waits for prey that it can quickly grab. Once it has prey, it squeezes — or constricts — the prey until the prey can't breathe anymore. The boa constrictor eats the prey once it has died.

Is the boa constrictor an apex predator then?

Jaguars (said this way: jăg-wåhrs) and crocodiles hunt boa constrictors, so they are not apex predators. The jaguar is a large, spotted cat. It can often be found among the branches of the understory, where it waits for prey. Once it spots its prey, the jaguar will jump from the branches and catch it by surprise. The jaguar is an apex predator in the jungle.

 The jaguar is one of the largest cats in the world. Their beautiful dark spots are called rosettes, and they help to camouflage the jaguar in its environment. Color the picture of a jaguar and her cubs.

 Use a tape measure to measure 10 feet, the length of some boa constrictors. What do you think it would be like to find a snake that long in the rainforest?

The rainforest understory is an interesting place! Another one of my favorite creatures lives in the understory: the red-eyed tree frog. The red-eyed tree frog is an amphibian, like the poison dart frog.

The red-eyed tree frog is so colorful! Bright colors are usually a signal to predators that a creature is venomous or poisonous. Are red-eyed tree frogs poisonous, like poison dart frogs?

They aren't poisonous, actually! The red-eyed tree frog uses its bright coloring to shock and scare predators like birds or bats. When the red-eyed tree frog is sleeping, its bright eyes are closed, and it tucks its feet under its body to hide them. Since the bright colors are hidden, the frog's green body is camouflaged on the tree.

If a predator finds it, the red-eyed tree frog will open its eyes and quickly move its bright feet. The flash of color will scare the predator.

Those bright red eyes would shock me if I wasn't expecting them!

While the predator is surprised, and wondering if this prey is poisonous, the red-eyed tree frog will quickly hop away to safety.

I think their bright coloring shows God's creativity, but that's not the only way He created the red-eyed tree frog uniquely. We use suction cups to hold our washcloths in the shower — but did you know God invented the suction cup first? God gave the red-eyed tree frog sticky suction cups on their toes. This enables the frog to climb quickly and easily through the rainforest.

Whoa, that is really neat!

The red-eyed tree frog is **nocturnal** (said this way: nŏc-ter-nl), which means it sleeps during the day and is active at night. It is also a carnivore. The red-eyed tree frog eats flies, moths, other insects, and sometimes other small frogs. It is important to the rainforest because it helps to keep the number of insects from becoming too large. The red-eyed tree frog helps to keep the rainforest in balance.

 Tell your teacher how a red-eyed tree frog uses its bright colors to protect itself from predators.

 Mosquitos and moths are common in the tropical rainforest. You can learn more about them in *God's Big Book of Animals*.

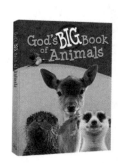

I've had fun learning about the rainforest's understory and a little about the creatures that live there. I noticed, though, that the jaguar and the boa constrictor wait for prey to come by, and then they sneak up on it and surprise it.

Predators often lie in wait for their prey. Did you know that the Bible compares Satan and temptation to predators? Temptation is the desire to do something that is wrong. Sometimes, it can feel like temptation sneaks up on us.

I felt like that yesterday! I was walking through the kitchen, and I saw a piece of candy sitting on the countertop. It wasn't mine, but all of a sudden, I really wanted to take it. I felt like temptation had snuck up on me and I wanted to do something I knew was wrong.

What did you do?

I remembered 1 Corinthians 10:13 (NIrV):

You are tempted in the same way all other human beings are. God is faithful. He will not let you be tempted any more than you can take. But when you are tempted, God will give you a way out. Then you will be able to deal with it.

I wanted to take the piece of candy, but I knew it wasn't mine. Taking something that didn't belong to me would be stealing, so I prayed and asked God to help me do the right thing — and He did! I decided to walk out of the kitchen and go read a book instead.

You made a good choice! I'm so glad God doesn't leave us alone when we are tempted to do something wrong. When temptation comes, we can pray and ask Him for courage to make the right choice — even if it is hard.

I don't always make the right choice, though. God forgives us when we tell Him about what happened and ask for His forgiveness. God is faithful and merciful!

Day

We're wrapping up our exploration of the understory today, and we're ready to add a new page to our Science Notebook!

Ooh, can we draw a boa constrictor in our Notebooks today?

Yes, snakes are fun to draw because we can start with an S shape and then draw the rest of the snake. Here is an image we can use for an idea!

Perfect! Once we've drawn our snake, we can use this picture to help us color it in.

Here are our Notebooks. Have fun creating your own boa constrictor!

notebook

In your Science Notebook, write: **The boa constrictor is a non-venomous snake.**

Then, draw a picture of a boa constrictor.

Hidden Treasure

The boa constrictor and jaguar wait to surprise their prey. Sometimes, it can feel like temptation surprises us too. But 1 Corinthians 10:13 reminds us that God is faithful and He doesn't leave us alone when we are tempted. We can ask for His help to make the right choice. Copy 1 Corinthians 10:13b on the back of your Notebook page as a reminder.

But when you are tempted, God will give you a way out. Then you will be able to deal with it (1 Corinthians 10:13b).

Rainforest Floor

Day 1

Welcome back for another learning adventure in the tropical rainforest! We're almost done traveling through the rainforest's layers. What has been your favorite layer so far?

Mine was the canopy — I thought epiphytes were very interesting plants!

I enjoyed exploring the canopy and the creatures that live there as well! Now it's time to explore the last layer of the rainforest, the forest floor. I've been studying this layer, and I'd love to share what I've learned with you.

I'm excited to get started then!

When we explored the other layers of the tropical rainforest, we learned that they are full of plants, trees, and leaves.

Ooh, that reminds me — I have a new word for us. We can also call all those plants, trees, and leaves vegetation. **Vegetation** (said this way: vĕ-jĕ-tā-shŭn) is a big word that means plant and tree life in an area.

Thanks for sharing that with us, Ben! The forest floor is different from the other layers of the rainforest because very little sunlight can reach this layer through the thick vegetation above. The rainforest floor is a hot, dark layer. It is also damp. Damp is a word that means it isn't soaking wet, but it isn't dry either. If you touch something damp, it will feel slightly wet.

Like clothes that were washed, but haven't dried all the way yet. Or like the ground after a sprinkle of rain.

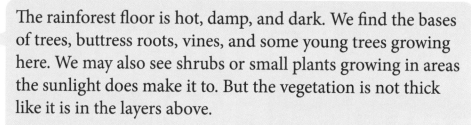

The rainforest floor is hot, damp, and dark. We find the bases of trees, buttress roots, vines, and some young trees growing here. We may also see shrubs or small plants growing in areas the sunlight does make it to. But the vegetation is not thick like it is in the layers above.

Tomorrow we'll learn more about the soil in the rainforest — I think you'll find it really interesting! But first, we still want to hear about your favorite layer of the rainforest!

 apply it — What layer of the rainforest has been your favorite to explore? What was your favorite part about it? Write your answer below.

_____

_____

_____

_____

_____

_____

_____

_____

_____

Day

After we studied the emergent layer, the canopy, and the understory, I thought that the soil in the rainforest would have many nutrients for all the plants that grow.

Hmm, that would make sense. We call soil that has many nutrients available rich, fertile soil.

I've learned though that the soil in rainforests usually isn't rich and fertile. Instead, it is often quite acidic and low in nutrients.

Wait, I'm confused. How do so many plants and trees grow well in the rainforest then? They all need many nutrients to be available.

Great question! Let's look at how the tropical rainforest is designed to find the answer. Remember what we learned about decomposition when we explored the deciduous forest? Decomposition is the process in which dead plants and animals break back down into the soil. Decomposition returns nutrients to the soil.

In the tropical rainforest, dead plant and animal material usually falls to the forest floor. Material can decompose quickly in damp and dark environments — which is exactly what the rainforest floor is. The forest floor is also home to a variety of mushrooms, fungi, insects, and types of bacteria that help material to decay quickly.

And as that material decays, it returns nutrients to the soil that plants and animals use.

In the deciduous forest, material can take a long time to decay. But the process is much faster in the tropical rainforest because it is damp and dark. This allows nutrients to return to the soil faster so that plants can use them.

So, decomposition keeps nutrients available for the plants and trees that grow in the rainforest.

Exactly! But there is still more to the design in the rainforest. We'll talk more about it tomorrow. First, there are many types of fungus that grow in the tropical rainforest. Many types are beautiful. Let's look at some!

 applyit Copy the name of each fungi below.

Bridal Veil Stinkhorn

Anemone Stinkhorn

Indigo Milk Cap

Arched Sawgill

I thought it was really interesting how decomposition returns nutrients quickly to the soil in the tropical rainforest. What a great design! But you mentioned yesterday that it isn't the only design that helps the rainforest thrive. Can you tell us more, Hannah?

Nutrients return to the soil quickly in the tropical rainforest — but there is another problem. Nutrients are also used up quickly by other plants and animals. This means that nutrients won't sink deeply into the soil the way they do in the deciduous forest.

Uh-oh, that sounds like a problem for the trees. Their roots need to be able to absorb nutrients from within the soil.

In the deciduous forest, a tree sends its roots deep into the soil. In the tropical rainforest, however, a tree's roots will stay near the surface of the soil. This allows the roots to absorb the nutrients there quickly, which is important since the roots may not be able to receive nutrients in deep soil.

Do you remember when we talked about buttress roots? Buttress roots give a tall tree a sturdy foundation above the surface. This allows trees to keep their root system near the surface of the soil, rather than deep within the ground. Without buttress roots, the tree would need to grow its roots deep in order to anchor it firmly in place.

What an amazing design! I've enjoyed seeing how God created a diverse number of plants, trees, and animals that can live in different biomes. For example, some trees are designed to thrive in the deciduous forest — but they wouldn't do very well in the tropical rainforest. This shows me God's wisdom and creativity.

God's creative and diverse designs give us many different environments, habitats, and biomes to explore and enjoy. Each area has amazing plants, creatures, and relationships that God put in place.

Creatures! That reminds me, we haven't learned about any creatures that live on the forest floor yet.

Don't worry! I've been learning about one creature and I'll share all about it in our next adventure.

apply it — What do you think the world would be like if there were not different kinds of trees, plants, animals, and biomes? Write your answer below.

The Bengal tiger can live in some parts of the rainforest. You can learn more about tigers in *God's Big Book of Animals*.

We're almost done learning about the rainforest floor, but first I'm ready to hear about the creature you've been learning about Ben!

There are many kinds of termites, beetles, spiders, and ants that live on the rainforest floor. In fact, there can be millions of insects in the rainforest! One very interesting insect is the leaf-cutter ant.

In the Amazon rainforest, you may find long lines of leaf-cutter ants carrying pieces of leaves. God designed this ant with strong, scissor-like jaws that can quickly slice through leaves and flowers. Leaf-cutter ants will cut a piece of leaf that may weigh far more than they do — but they carry it with ease.

What do they do with all of those cut-up leaves?

You might think the ants eat the leaves, but they don't! Leaf-cutter ants eat fungus — a special fungus that grows on top of the leaf pieces they've cut.

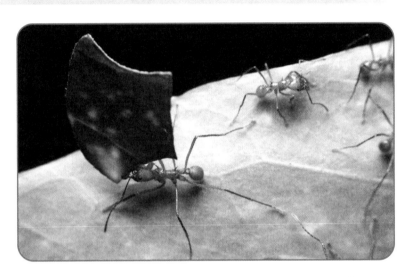

Leaf-cutter ants live under the forest floor in long tunnels and chambers. We call this a colony, and there can be over a million ants all living together in the colony! The leaf-cutter ant carries the leaf pieces into the colony. There, the ants will prepare the leaves so that fungus can grow on them. The ants will protect and care for the fungus, just like a farmer cares for their crops.

What hard workers! Did you know that the Bible mentions the ant in Proverbs 6:6–8? Let's read it together,

Go to the ant, you sluggard; consider its ways and be wise! It has no commander, no overseer or ruler, yet it stores its provisions in summer and gathers its food at harvest.

Sluggard is a word that means a person who is lazy, or who doesn't want to work. When we look at the ants, each ant has a job to do. The ant works diligently — or steadily — at its job. Because of its hard work, the ant takes care of itself and others. Ants remind us that we can work diligently too in whatever job we are given to do.

We're almost ready to begin creating our tropical rainforest biome — but first, we have one more page to add to our Science Notebook!

Ooh, can we add a leaf-cutter ant? We can use this picture to give us an idea of what to draw in our Notebooks. We can draw just a few leaf-cutter ants, or a whole line of them.

Great idea! We can draw three small circles for the body of our ant, and then add the legs. Don't forget to add some leaf pieces too!

Here's what our Notebooks look like! Have fun creating your drawing. We'll start creating our model biome in our next lesson. It's going to be so much fun!

In your Science Notebook, write: **Leaf-cutter ants gather leaves to grow fungus on.**

Then, draw a picture of leaf-cutter ants carrying leaves.

We learned about the rainforest floor and the leaf-cutter ant this week. The leaf-cutter ant works hard, and it is a reminder that we can also work diligently in whatever job we are given to do. Copy Proverbs 6:6 on the back of your Notebook page as a reminder.

Go to the ant, you sluggard; consider its ways and be wise (Proverbs 6:6)!

Rainforest Biome Project

I don't know about you, but I sure had a lot of fun learning about the tropical rainforest biome! I also enjoyed seeing the different ways God designed plants and creatures to live in this biome.

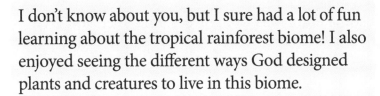

I did too! I'm most excited about creating our own model biome of the tropical rainforest, though.

I knew you would be. I've got our shoebox here all ready to go. Mom thought we should paint our background for the tropical rainforest.

Ooh, painting? This should be fun! What do we need to paint first?

The tropical rainforest has a lot of green due to all the plants. Let's paint the sides, top, and back of the shoebox green first. Then we'll add more to our biome each day this week.

materials needed

- [ ] Acrylic paint set
- [ ] Tablecloth to protect table
- [ ] Paintbrushes
- [ ] Shoebox

Activity directions:

1. Spread out a tablecloth to protect the table.

2. Use green acrylic paint to paint the inside of your shoebox. You'll want to paint the back, top, and sides green.

3. Put the shoebox in a safe place to dry. We'll add more tomorrow!

4. Carefully rinse out your paintbrush.

> I've got our model biome here. What are we going to add today?

Our background looks nice and green — now it's time to add some trees or bushes. We can paint tall trees on the back and sides of our shoebox.

Ooh, we can add some epiphytes to the trees, and even some vines winding their way up the tree!

Great ideas, Ben! I've got a few paint colors here for us to use. We'll need to rinse out our paintbrush before we change paint colors. We can dry the brush on the paper towel before we dip it into the next paint color.

Let's get started!

Activity directions:

1. Spread out a tablecloth to protect the table.

2. Begin painting trees on your biome. You can start by painting the trunks and branches. Then rinse the paintbrush in the water and dry it on the paper towel.

3. Next, paint leaves on the tree. You'll need a darker green paint color than the background is. You can paint green circles at the end of your branches, or paint smaller groups of leaves if you'd like.

4. Rinse your paintbrush and choose the next color. Now you can paint some epiphytes or vines on your trees!

5. Once you're done painting, carefully rinse out the paintbrush. Put the shoebox in a safe place to dry. We'll add more tomorrow!

materials needed

- [ ] Acrylic paint set
- [ ] Tablecloth to protect table
- [ ] Paintbrushes
- [ ] Bowl of water
- [ ] Paper towels

Day

It has been so much fun creating our tropical rainforest biome! Let's create the ground today. We can paint the bottom of the box brown.

Can I paint a river through our biome?

Sure! I'll paint the brown dirt and vines, and you can paint the river. Oh, you can also paint some green along the bottom edge of our box. Let's start painting!

Activity directions:

materials needed

- ☐ Acrylic paint set
- ☐ Tablecloth to protect table
- ☐ Paintbrushes
- ☐ Bowl of water
- ☐ Paper towels

1. Spread out a tablecloth to protect the table.

2. Paint the bottom of the shoebox brown. Rinse out the paintbrush and then let the brown dry for a bit.

3. Once the brown is dry to the touch, you can begin painting a river through your biome if you'd like.

4. You can also paint long, winding vines along your rainforest floor.

5. Once you're done painting, carefully rinse out the paintbrush. Put the shoebox in a safe place to dry. We'll add more tomorrow!

I love the river you painted through our model rainforest biome, Ben!

Thanks! Today is the day it'll really start coming together — we need to add some more trees. I have an idea for how to add buttress roots to our trees too!

Ooh, I can't wait to get started. I have the trees we made for our deciduous biome. We can re-use those trees.

materials needed

☐ Trees from the deciduous biome

☐ Brown construction paper

☐ Tape

☐ Scissors

☐ Twine or yarn

☐ Hot glue gun or mini glue dots

Activity directions:

1. If you no longer have the trees that were created for the deciduous biome, you can make new trees following that same process.

2. Fold the brown construction paper in half. Cut a semi-oval from the paper to create 2 equal pieces.

3. Cut the bottom of one semi-oval so that the cut is about ¼ inch from the top. Cut the second semi-oval from the top so that the cut is about ¼ inch from the bottom.

4. Slide the cut slits of the semi-ovals over each other to create a buttress root base.

5. If you are re-using the deciduous trees, remove the playdough base. Tape the bottom of the dowel to the buttress root base.

6. Cut pieces of twine to attach to the biome ceiling. These will be our vines. Use mini glue dots or a hot glue gun (adult only!) to attach the ends of the twine to the shoebox's ceiling.

7. Place the biome in a safe place; we'll be finishing it tomorrow!

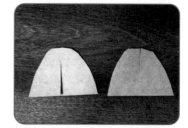

Our biome looks so good — but it's missing one important part! We're ready to add some small model birds and animals to our biome today. If you don't have any, you can also use playdough to create some or ask your teacher to help you find and print some pictures you can use. Let's add our animals to the rainforest model!

Activity directions:

materials needed

☐ Small rainforest animals like toucan, snake, tiger, frog, monkey, etc.

☐ Mini glue dots

1. Add the small animals to your tropical rainforest biome model. If you'd like, you can use mini glue dots to attach some creatures, like frogs, higher in the biome. You can also let animals swing from the vines.

2. Share your biome with your family. Be sure to tell them what you've learned about the tropical rainforest and God's design.

Bonus! Take a picture of your tropical rainforest biome and ask your teacher to help you print it out. Then, tape or glue the picture on the next page in your Science Notebook. Write **My Tropical Rainforest Biome** at the top of the page.

applyit Color this picture of a toucan from the tropical rainforest.

The Grassland

Day

Welcome back, friend! Can you believe we've already explored three of the earth's biomes? I really enjoyed learning about the boreal forest, deciduous forest, and tropical rainforest with you. As we've explored these biomes, we've also found many elements of God's design.

You're right, when we investigate and explore God's creation, we see His wisdom and design all around. That is what I love most about science. Today, we'll begin exploring the grassland biome. Let's get started!

Hmm, grassland — it sounds like this biome will have a lot of grass?

That is correct! The most common type of vegetation in this biome is grass. There are many different types of grasses, and we'll be talking more about a few types soon. First, let's learn a little more about the grassland biome.

Grasslands are one of the earth's largest biomes. They can be found all around the world. We organize grasslands into two different types: temperate grasslands and tropical grasslands. Temperate grasslands can be found in North and South America, Asia, Australia, and Europe.

Temperate grasslands can have different names, depending on where they are found. Temperate grasslands in North America are called **prairies** (said this way: pr-air-rēs). In South America, they are called **pampas** (said this way: păm-pŭz). In Europe and Asia, temperate grasslands are called **steppes** (said this way: stěps). Temperate grasslands usually receive about 10–30 inches of rain each year.

Wow! Rainforests can receive around 80 inches of rain each year. When you compare that to the grassland, the grassland is a much drier place. What is the climate like in the temperate grassland?

Depending on where the grassland is located in the world, the summers in this biome can be very warm. Some areas may even reach over 100° Fahrenheit! The winters are quite cold. The temperatures can often reach far below freezing. Some areas may also receive snow!

I'm excited to learn more about grasslands. But first, let's look at some pictures of a few different grasslands.

 Copy the name of each type of grassland below.

prairie

_____

- - - - - - - - - - - - - - - - - -

_____

pampas

_____

- - - - - - - - - - - - - - - - - -

_____

steppe

_____

- - - - - - - - - - - - - - - - - -

_____

Do you see anything that is similar in each type of grassland? Tell your teacher what is similar and what is different in each type.

We talked about temperate grasslands yesterday. Can we talk about tropical grasslands today? I'm excited to learn more about those since we just finished exploring the tropical rainforest. Are tropical grasslands wet and rainy, like tropical rainforests?

Actually, no. Unlike the tropical rainforest, tropical grasslands are dry places.

Hmm, now I have a question. If tropical grasslands are drier, like temperate grasslands, why do we call them tropical?

I'm glad you asked! The word tropical tells us where we find these grasslands. Just like the tropical rainforest, tropical grasslands are located around the equator. Tropical grasslands are also called savannahs.

Over our next few lessons, we're going to closely explore the savannah in Africa. Africa is a continent. Savannahs can also be found on the continents of Australia, South America, and in Southern Asia.

Wait — let's talk about what a continent is first. When you look at a globe of the earth, you may notice that the land is broken up into large pieces. We call a large area of land a **continent** (said this way: kŏn-tĕ-nĕnt). There are seven continents on earth. The continents are Africa, Asia, Antarctica, Europe, Australia, North America, and South America.

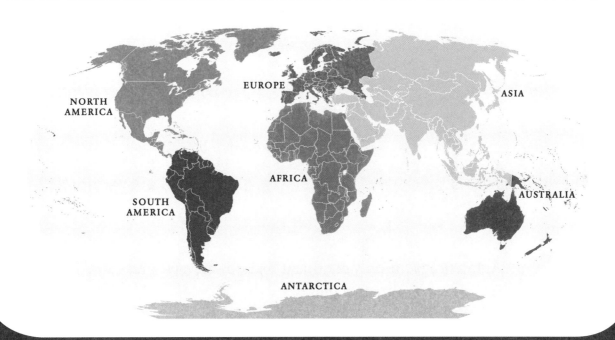

Thanks, Ben! Africa is one of the seven continents, and much of it is covered by savannah. Though the savannah is much drier than the tropical rainforest, it does have a wet season and a dry season like the rainforest.

How much rain does the savannah usually receive?

Depending on the location, a savannah may receive about 20–50 inches annually. **Annually** (said this way: ăn-yoo-ŭh-lē) is another word we can use to say "each year."

Most of the rain will come during the wet season, which can last between 6–8 months in the savannah. During this season, many different types of grasses can grow thick and plentiful. Their roots will grow deep into the soil as they prepare for the dry season. We'll talk more about the dry season tomorrow!

apply it

Write the missing word in each sentence:

wet   savannahs   continent   Africa

1. A large area of land is called a _____.

2. Tropical grasslands are also called _____.

3. Much of _____ is covered by the savannah biome.

4. The savannah has a _____ season and a dry season.

Antarctica is the only continent that doesn't have grassland. Locate Antarctica on a map or globe.

Welcome back, friend! We learned about the savannah's wet season yesterday. Let's learn about the dry season today! Hannah, how long does the dry season last?

Depending on where the savannah is located, the dry season can last for 4–6 months. During that time there may be no rain at all, or only a very small amount.

Wow, that is a long time without rain! The plants and trees growing in the savannah grassland need water, though. How are they able to continue living for such a long time without rain?

Hmm, let me ask you a question first. As we've studied the biomes, have you noticed that the plants and trees that grow in each biome are well designed to live there?

I have! They each have unique parts of their design, like a waxy coating to keep water from evaporating away or leaves that fall from the tree before winter.

Right! God designed plants, trees, and animals with the ability to adapt. **Adapt** (said this way: ŭh-dăpt) means to adjust or change for certain conditions or a particular environment.

For example, in a wet climate like the rainforest, a tree's roots stay closer to the surface of the soil because water is plentiful. But in a dry climate, a tree will adapt and grow its roots deep within the soil. This allows the tree to reach water far below the surface.

I see God's wisdom in that! Without the ability to adapt to different conditions, we wouldn't see a diverse number of plants, trees, and animals in all different biomes.

God designed creation with the ability to adapt, and that is what allows trees and plants to grow even in a dry environment. In the savannah, grasses grow their roots deep within the soil. We'll be talking more about the design of savannah grass soon!

applyit What does the word adapt mean?

I'm looking forward to learning more about the savannah, especially grass, as we continue our adventure!

Me too! In the meantime, though, I was thinking about the plants and animals that live in the savannah during the dry season. The plants must adapt to survive with little or no rain, and the animals must search for water to drink. Sometimes, water must be very hard to find, and I'm sure they get quite thirsty!

The dry season reminded me of what King David wrote in Psalm 63:1:

You, God, are my God, earnestly I seek you; I thirst for you, my whole being longs for you, in a dry and parched land where there is no water.

I remember when Mom told us about that verse. David wrote these words while he was hiding in the desert. The desert is another biome that is even drier than the savannah. I wonder if David happened to see an animal searching for water before he wrote those words? Or maybe even David himself was very thirsty in that dry land.

I wondered that too! Earnest is a word that means to be serious in what we do, to be diligent, or to do something with purpose. If we were in a dry land, we would be diligent in searching for water.

In the same way, the world around us can be like a hot, dry desert. It leaves our hearts thirsty — but only Jesus can satisfy that thirst. We must earnestly seek and desire the Lord, just as King David did.

Sometimes, it is easy to get distracted by other things and forget to seek the Lord. But the more I spend time with God reading the Bible, learning about Him, and praying, the more I also desire to do those things. Thanks for sharing with us today, Ben!

Day

I'm so glad you're here now — it's my favorite day!
Let's add a new page to our Science Notebook.

Let's draw a picture of a savannah grassland. We can
use this picture to give us an idea for what to draw.

This is going to
be fun!

Here is what
each of our
savannahs
look like. Have
fun creating
your own
drawing, and
don't forget
to show it to
someone else!

In your Science Notebook, write: **Tropical grasslands are called savannahs.**

Then, draw a picture of the savannah.

Learning about the dry season this week also reminded us that we must seek God, just as we would seek water in a dry land. Copy Psalm 63:1 on the back of your Notebook page as a reminder.

You, God, are my God, earnestly I seek you; I thirst for you, my whole being longs for you, in a dry and parched land where there is no water (Psalm 63:1).

Savannah Grasses

**Day**

Hello, friend! Are you ready to continue exploring the savannah with us?

I know I am! It's time to learn more about the grasses that grow in the savannah.

It sure is — I've been reading all about savannah grass, and I have a lot to share with you. Grass is a type of plant that can be found growing all over the world. There are thousands of different species of grass. Hannah, you might be surprised to learn that the rice we had with dinner last night grows from a type of grass!

Really? That is interesting!

And don't forget about the oatmeal we ate this morning! Oats also grow on a type of grass. Grass provides an important source of food for both people and animals. That is one reason grasslands are an important biome!

One thing that makes grass a unique type of plant is that it can continue to grow even after being cut down or eaten by an animal.

That makes sense. The yard around our house is covered with grass. Dad mows the grass each week during the summer to keep it from growing too tall. Once it is mowed, though, it doesn't take long for the grass to grow right back — sometimes even taller than it was before it was mowed!

The ability to grow back quickly is an important feature of grass. We're going to be talking more about it as we continue exploring the savannah!

applyit There are many different types of grass. Copy the name of each type below.

Lemongrass

Wheat

Barley

Timothy

Kentucky bluegrass

I'm looking forward to learning more about grasses today. We've talked a little about the dry season in the savannah. Can you tell us more about how grass is able to survive with no, or very little, water during that season?

I sure can! As we talked about before, God designed much of creation with the ability to adapt. The trees and plants that grow in the savannah have adapted to be able to handle drought.

Don't forget, the word drought means a long period of time without rain.

In the savannah, some types of grasses have adapted by growing their roots deep into the soil. This allows them to reach water that may be available far beneath the surface. Other types of grasses have adapted in a different way — their roots don't grow as deep. Instead, the roots grow into a big, tangled mess.

Hmm, I understand how long, deep roots help the grass reach water. But how do tangled roots help the grass to receive the water it needs?

I was hoping you'd ask! These tangled roots hold the soil together tightly — kind of like if you were to hold soil tightly in your fist. Water tends to get trapped in the tight soil around the tangled roots. This keeps water available for the grass longer than it would if the roots stayed spread out and water drained through.

Another way some types of grass survive the dry season is that the plant will dry out above the surface of the soil. In other words, the grass plant becomes dormant. **Dormant** (said this way: dōr-měnt) means resting, not active or growing.

Like deciduous trees during the winter!

Exactly! On the surface, it may even look like the brown, withered grass has died. But beneath the surface, the roots are still alive. Once it rains, the grass will begin to grow thick and plentiful again.

applyit In the savannah, grass can grow roots that are deep or tangled. How do long, deep roots help grass receive water?

How do tangled roots help grass receive water?

 If you have grass around your house, ask your teacher for permission to dig up a little of the plant. What do the roots look like? Are they short or do they extend far into the soil?

I'd love to learn more about some of the types of grasses we may see growing in the savannah. Can you tell us more, Ben?

That sounds like fun! Since the savannah covers such a large area, there are many different kinds of grasses that grow here. Some common types of grass we may see in the savannah are Rhodes, red oats, Bermuda, and elephant grass.

Rhodes grass is an important part of the food chain in areas of the savannah. In order to survive during the dry season, Rhodes grass grows a long root deep into the soil. This type of root is called a **taproot**, and it helps the plant reach the water it needs. Smaller roots may also branch out from the taproot.

Before we learn more about grass, we need to talk again about fire. Do you remember when we learned about the boreal forest? We learned that fire is destructive in the boreal forest biome, but it also helps to clean the forest and return nutrients to the soil.

Grass fires are also an important part of the savannah. During the dry season, grasses dry out. Older grasses die, and dead material begins to build up on the dirt. As more and more dead grass material builds up over time, it makes it difficult for living plants to receive the sunlight and water they need to grow.

Grass fires can sweep quickly through an area of the savannah and burn away the old, dead material. This returns nutrients to the soil and opens space for new plants to grow. Though a grass fire burns away some of the living grass too, the roots stay safe under the dirt. Once the fire is over, the grass will begin growing again.

Red oats grass is a very common type of grass in the savannah. It keeps seeds under the surface of the dirt to protect them from fire. This type of grass can grow quickly after a fire and is also an important part of the food chain.

applyit — Copy the name of each type of grass below.

Rhodes grass

red oats grass

Bermuda grass

elephant grass

Day

I've enjoyed learning more about the types of grasses we see in the savannah! We still have two types that we haven't talked about — Bermuda grass and elephant grass. I'd love to hear more about those types!

Let's dig right in! Bermuda grass is another common type of grass in the savannah. This type of grass creates a dense covering and can grow to be around 16 inches tall. Its roots travel deep into the soil. During the dry season, the top of the grass will dry out and die — but the roots stay alive beneath the ground.

Elephant grass can grow quite tall, up to 10 feet! This type of grass is rough and can have sharp edges. These features discourage many herbivores from eating it, though elephants do enjoy munching on this type of grass.

There are so many different types of grasses, and they impact their environment in different ways. I think it is amazing how God designed so many different types of grasses to provide food for people and animals.

I agree! I've been thinking a lot about grass as we've been learning over the last few days. Even though grass can continue growing after being cut or eaten, it does eventually die, and new grass will take its place. It reminds me of the verse we learned on Sunday — Isaiah 40:8:

The grass withers and the flowers fall, but the word of our God endures forever.

I was thinking of that verse too! In creation, we see many things that wither and fade away. Even the beautiful flowers only last a short while. But God's Word endures forever. That means it never fails or disappears — we can trust it.

What a great reminder from grass!

We're all ready to add a new page to our Science Notebooks today! What do you think we should draw today, Ben?

Hmm, we learned about a few different types of grasses this week. Let's draw a picture of Bermuda grass, Rhodes grass, and elephant grass to remind us that God created many different types of grass.

Okay, that sounds like fun! We can use these pictures to help us draw each type.

Bermuda grass

Rhodes grass

elephant grass

Here is what each of our Notebooks looks like. Have fun creating yours!

notebook

In your Notebook, draw a picture of Bermuda grass and write **Bermuda grass** to label the picture. Next, draw a picture of Rhodes grass and write **Rhodes grass** to label the picture. Finally, draw a picture of elephant grass and write **elephant grass** to label the picture.

Learning about grass this week also reminded us that the grass may wither, but God's Word lasts forever. Copy Isaiah 40:8 on the back of your Notebook page as a reminder.

The grass withers and the flowers fall, but the word of our God endures forever (Isaiah 40:8).

Acacia Trees

Day

Welcome back, friend! We've been exploring the savannah grassland together, and I'm excited to learn more today! You know, we've talked a lot about trees in each of the other biomes we studied. The boreal forest, deciduous forest, and tropical rainforest biomes all have many, many trees. The grassland biome is different, though, because there are not many trees in this one. Can you tell us why, Hannah?

Absolutely! There are a couple of reasons why we don't see as many trees in grasslands. The first reason is that there usually just isn't enough water to support many trees. In order for a forest to grow, there needs to be plenty of water available for all of the trees. Grasslands, however, usually receive less rain than forests.

So that means there typically isn't enough water available to support many trees growing in the same area of grassland.

Correct. In the savannah, trees tend to grow scattered across the land instead of grouped closely together. Because the trees are scattered, they do not create a forest canopy as the trees do in a forest. We call the grassland an open canopy because there is not a forest canopy that blocks the sunlight.

Ah, and an open canopy is very important to grasslands because this allows sunlight to reach the grassy vegetation. What is the second reason, Hannah?

The second reason trees are scattered throughout the savannah is fire. When there is enough rain in the savannah, trees may begin growing close together. If they continue growing closely, a canopy will form over time. This would cause the biome to change from a grassland to a forest.

Many people and animals rely on grasslands, though. Just like in the boreal forest, fire is important to keep a grassland healthy. Fire will kill young trees and prevent them from growing closely together. However, the older and taller trees are often resistant to fire and can withstand the heat from the flames.

Wow, I definitely see God's wisdom and design in the way the older, taller trees are able to withstand fire.

applyit

A grassland has an open canopy because the trees typically grow scattered apart from each other. What are two reasons why trees grow scattered throughout the savannah? Write your answer below.

_____

_____

_____

_____

_____

_____

_____

_____

We're back and ready to learn more about trees in the savannah!

Oh, good. I've been learning about two of the trees we see in the savannah, and I'd love to share what I've learned with you! Let's start with the acacia (said this way: ŭh-kāy-shǔ). Acacias are a family group of trees that include many types of trees and shrubs. Two types of acacia that we see in the savannah are the umbrella thorn acacia and the whistling thorn acacia.

The umbrella thorn acacia is a common sight in much of the African savannah. This tree grows a long taproot to help it reach water stored deep underground. The branches and leaves of this tree spread out tall and wide, giving it the shape of an umbrella.

One interesting feature of the umbrella thorn acacia tree is its ability to protect itself from herbivores. The savannah is the home of large herbivores like elephants and giraffes. Both of these creatures can consume a lot of leaves each day. If a giraffe or elephant ate too many leaves from a tree, the tree wouldn't be able to photosynthesize well enough, and it could die.

The umbrella thorn acacia tree grows long, sharp thorns that help keep herbivores from eating too many leaves.

Ouch! Thorns would definitely keep me from eating leaves off of a tree.

Hmm, I don't know about that! Mom's raspberry bushes have thorns — but you love raspberries too much to not pick and eat them.

Okay, you're right. But I pick them very slowly and carefully so that I don't get hurt.

And that is exactly how some herbivores handle the prickly umbrella thorn acacia tree. The sharp thorns discourage most herbivores from eating the leaves. But, if an animal does decide to risk the thorns and eats the acacia leaves anyway, the thorns make sure the animal eats the leaves slowly and carefully. This protects the tree from too many leaves being eaten quickly all at once.

Neat! I don't really like thorns, but it is amazing how God gave even thorns a purpose in creation.

 The giraffe loves to carefully eat leaves from the umbrella thorn acacia tree. Color the giraffe picture below.

Yesterday we learned how thorns help to keep herbivores from eating too many leaves from the umbrella thorn acacia tree. But that actually isn't the only way this tree discourages creatures from eating too many leaves!

When an animal, like a giraffe, begins eating from an acacia tree, the leaves release a chemical toxin. The toxin makes the leaves taste bad, and it can also make the animal sick.

Which means the animal won't want to eat the leaves anymore!

The tree's ability to release a toxin helps keep herbivores from eating too much. But it still doesn't end there!

Some types of acacias were also created with a way to warn other acacias near them that a hungry herbivore is ready to eat. When an animal begins eating its leaves, the tree releases the chemical toxin into the leaves. The tree can also release another chemical — this chemical causes other acacia trees nearby to also release the chemical toxin into their leaves.

So once the creature realizes it can't eat the acacia leaves in that area it will move on! I think it's amazing that God gave these trees a way to protect themselves from having too many of their leaves eaten. Hannah, you also mentioned the whistling acacia. Can you tell us about that one?

The whistling acacia also has thorns — but underneath the thorns are hollow balls called bulbs. The bulbs have holes in them from insects that have eaten through. When the wind blows through the holes in the bulbs, it makes a whistling sound — that is how this tree got its name!

The whistling acacia doesn't release a toxin into its tiny leaves. Instead, it relies on mutualism to help keep it protected. Stinging ants make their home in the bulbs of the whistling acacia tree. If another creature comes to eat from the tree, the ants will swarm over the creature to defend their home. Nobody likes to be swarmed by ants!

The tree provides a home and food for the ants, and the ants help defend the tree from other herbivores.

applyit God designed the umbrella thorn acacia tree with thorns and a chemical toxin to help keep herbivores from eating too many leaves from the tree. He also designed a symbiotic relationship for the whistling acacia. If you could create a tree, what ways would you give it to protect itself from herbivores in the savannah? Tell your teacher how your tree would protect itself.

As we learned about the umbrella thorn acacia tree's thorns, it reminded me of thorns in the Bible. Did you know thorns are mentioned at the beginning of the Bible, in Genesis? After Adam and Eve sinned, God told them the consequences of their disobedience. Creation would no longer be perfect, the way He had originally created it. In Genesis 3:17–18, God said,

Cursed is the ground because of you; through painful toil you will eat food from it all the days of your life. It will produce thorns and thistles for you, and you will eat the plants of the field.

Thorns and thistles were part of the consequences of sin. But, they also give a plant a way to defend itself in an imperfect world, which reveals God's wisdom and mercy.

Adam and Eve's sin broke God's original, perfect creation. Sin always has sad consequences. It always destroys. And worst of all, our sin separates us from God because He is holy and perfect. Thorns are a reminder that the world is broken by sin, and our relationship with God was also broken by sin.

But that isn't the end of the story! When Jesus came to the earth, He lived a life without sin. Jesus came to redeem us — to pay the price of sin for us. Though Jesus was innocent, John 19:2–3 says,

The soldiers twisted together a crown of thorns and put it on his head. They clothed him in a purple robe and went up to him again and again, saying, "Hail, king of the Jews!" And they slapped him in the face.

Thorns are a reminder of sin's ugly, painful consequences. As Jesus paid the price for our sin, He wore a crown of thorns. Jesus' painful crown of thorns reminds us that He carried and paid for our sin — even though He didn't have to. John 3:16 tells us,

For God so loved the world that he gave his one and only Son, that whoever believes in him shall not perish but have eternal life.

Because Jesus paid the price of sin, it can no longer separate us from God when we believe in Jesus. Thorns always remind me of sin's consequences. But they also remind me that Jesus paid the price of sin for me so that I can spend all of eternity — all of forever — with Him.

If you would like to believe and trust in Jesus, be sure to talk about it with your parent or teacher.

It's time for my favorite day!

I didn't think it was your birthday yet?

Oh, Hannah, you're so funny. My birthday is one of my favorite days, but I'm not talking about that one. I'm talking about the day we add a new page to our Science Notebook!

Oh, right! Wasn't it interesting to learn about the ways God designed acacia trees? Let's draw a picture of an umbrella thorn acacia tree in our Science Notebook. I have a picture that we can use for an example; here it is!

I love drawing trees; here is what ours look like!

In your Science Notebook, write: **The umbrella thorn acacia tree can be found in the African savannah.**

Then, draw a picture of an umbrella thorn acacia tree.

 Learning about thorns this week also reminded us that Jesus wore a crown of thorns as He paid for sin for us. Copy John 3:16 on the back of your Notebook page as a reminder.

For God so loved the world that he gave his one and only Son, that whoever believes in him shall not perish but have eternal life (John 3:16).

The Elephant

Day

I'm so excited you're here! Ben and I were just getting ready to begin our science adventure today. We're going to talk about a really big animal this week. In fact, this animal is also known as the largest mammal that lives on land.

Hmm, is it a giraffe?

That's a good guess, but no. While the giraffe is the tallest mammal on land, it isn't the largest. The largest animal on land is the African elephant!

African elephants grow to be around 13 feet tall, and they are extremely heavy. We use the word "ton" to describe an elephant's weight. One ton equals 2,000 pounds. A small elephant may weigh only two tons. A very large elephant can weigh up to five tons!

Wow, that means an elephant can weigh 4,000 to 10,000 pounds!

Now, since the elephant is so big, you might think it also has rather loud footsteps. However, an elephant is able to walk very quietly because God designed the bottom of their feet with special padding.

Since the elephant is so heavy, all that weight creates a lot of pressure on their feet. All the pressure could make it painful for them to walk. The special padding gives their feet a cushion and also absorbs the sound of their footsteps.

That reminds me, I have a pair of sneakers that have a special cushion in them. It's like having a pillow in my shoe that supports my weight! When I need to do a lot of walking, those sneakers keep my feet comfortable all day long.

Elephants spend much of their time walking as they look for food and water. The cushion in your shoe works in a similar way to how the elephant's special padding works to keep them comfortable.

Isn't it fun when we see God's design in creation? Humans created cushioned sneakers, but God thought of it first! In His wisdom, God designed the elephant with a cushioned foot.

 applyit Elephants are very heavy animals! A small elephant can weigh 4,000 pounds — that is equal to two tons! If you weigh 50 pounds, it will take 80 of you to equal the weight of one small elephant. Ask your teacher to help you use a scale to see how much you weigh. Then, ask your teacher to divide 4,000 by your weight. How many of you would it take to equal the weight of one small elephant?

A large elephant can weigh 10,000 pounds. Ask your teacher to divide 10,000 by your weight. How many of you would it take to equal the weight of one large elephant?

Hello, friend! Wasn't it fun to learn a little about the African elephant and its cushioned feet yesterday? I'm excited to learn more about elephants now. Can we talk about an elephant's trunk today, Hannah?

I'm glad you asked! An elephant's trunk can be around 6 feet long. God designed their trunk with many thousands of muscles that can do both big and small jobs for the elephant.

When we were at the zoo during the summer, the zookeeper was helping the African elephant paint a picture. Do you remember how the zookeeper would dip the paintbrush into the paint, and then give the brush to the elephant? The elephant held the paintbrush in the tip of its trunk — kind of like I would hold a paintbrush with my hand! Then, the elephant moved its trunk back and forth over the paper.

I remember that! Elephants that are in captivity —

Captivity means that the animal is not free in the wild. Instead, people are taking care of the animal, as they do in a zoo for example.

Thanks, Ben! Elephants that are in captivity can be trained to do tricks, like painting pictures. Elephants are very smart creatures.

An elephant can use its trunk for very delicate jobs, like holding a paintbrush or picking a small leaf from a tree. Or the elephant can use its trunk for very big jobs like lifting heavy objects. In fact, the elephant's trunk can lift things that weigh several hundred pounds!

That is impressive! What else does its trunk do?

The elephant uses its trunk to suck up water. It can hold about 4–6 gallons of water in its trunk. It will then empty the water into its mouth to drink it. An elephant can also use its trunk to suck up dust and dirt from the savannah that it can spray over its body. The dust helps to protect the elephant's skin from sunburn and discourages insects from biting it.

Interesting! I'm sure glad we don't have to take dust showers when we go outside!

---

applyit The elephant can use its trunk to do many things. Write some things an elephant can do with its trunk below.

Use a tape measure to measure 6 feet, the length of an elephant's trunk.

Let's continue learning about elephants today! Did you know the African elephant is a keystone species? The African elephant is important to the savannah biome because it helps many other creatures, as well as the environment.

First, let's start with their tusks! Elephant tusks are the two strong, large teeth that grow beyond their mouth. An elephant's tusks continue growing throughout its life, and they are very useful tools.

Elephants are large animals, and they need plenty of water to drink. Water can be hard to find in the savannah, though. Sometimes, a creature must be able to find stored water underground. When water is hard to find, elephants use their tusks like a shovel to dig holes in the ground. If the elephant reaches stored water, the holes fill up with that water to create a small watering hole.

Other thirsty creatures — who may not be able to dig a hole themselves — can also drink from the hole.

God designed many relationships in creation. It's exciting to see how He designed some creatures to be able to help others. I see God's wisdom and care in this!

I do too! But we're not done yet. Elephants travel through the savannah with a group of other elephants.

We call a large group of the same type of animal a **herd** (said this way: hurd).

As a very large herbivore, an elephant can eat around 300 pounds of leaves, grasses, and fruit each day. Together, a herd of elephants can eat a lot of food! The elephants may eat smaller trees or trample them down. This keeps too many trees from growing in an area.

As a herd of elephants travel, they also create a path through the savannah. The elephant paths are an important way other creatures can travel through the savannah.

Kind of like how we use the roads to travel from one place to another. Without a road, traveling would be harder and take longer.

Exactly right. Elephants help other creatures in the savannah, and they help to maintain the grassland.

applyit Fill in each blank with the correct word:

herd   keystone   tusks

1. The elephant is a _____ species.

2. Elephants have _____, which are strong, large teeth.

3. A large group of the same type of animal is called a _____.

What do elephants do when they cannot find water?

_____

_____

_____

_____

_____

_____

_____

Day

We've had so much fun learning about elephants this week!

I agree, and I'm excited to continue exploring the savannah together. But first, there's another way elephants help the savannah that we didn't get to talk about yesterday.

Elephants are big creatures who produce a lot of waste. Their waste is called dung. As they walk through the savannah, elephants eat many different types of plants and seeds. The seeds travel through their digestive system and into the elephant's dung.

An elephant's dung provides nutrients for the seeds as they begin to grow. Since elephants walk through the savannah, they help to transport seeds to different areas.

Elephants help the savannah in so many ways! They help creatures find water, create pathways, keep too many trees from growing, and spread seeds throughout the savannah. It's no wonder they are a keystone species!

Indeed. Elephants are strong, powerful creatures, and they could use their strength to do more harm than good. But as a keystone species, we see elephants helping the savannah biome and the other creatures that live there.

The words we speak are also powerful. We can use them to build each other up or to hurt others. It reminds me of Ephesians 4:29,

Do not let any unwholesome talk come out of your mouths, but only what is helpful for building others up according to their needs, that it may benefit those who listen.

That is a great reminder, Hannah! Just as the elephant uses its strength to benefit others, we can choose to speak helpful words that build others up.

Do you know what day it is? It's the day we add another page to our Science Notebook!

Woohoo! Let's draw an elephant this week. Here is a picture we can use for an example.

Drawing elephants is fun! Here is what each of our elephants looks like. I love how each one is different!

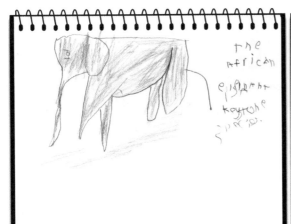

In your Science Notebook, write: **The African elephant is a keystone species.**

Then, draw a picture of an elephant.

Learning about how elephants help the savannah reminded us that we can also be sure to speak helpful words that help build others up. Copy Ephesians 4:29 on the back of your Notebook page as a reminder.

Do not let any unwholesome talk come out of your mouths, but only what is helpful for building others up according to their needs, that it may benefit those who listen (Ephesians 4:29).

Savannah Animals

Day

I really enjoyed learning about elephants in our last science adventure! I thought it would be fun to spend some time now learning about other animals that live in the savannah.

Ooh, that does sound like fun! What other animals live in the savannah?

The savannah is home to many different types of animals. Some are large, like elephants and giraffes, while others are small, like meerkats. There are predators like lions and cheetahs, as well as herbivores like antelope and zebras.

I was looking at some pictures from the savannah this morning, and I noticed that many types of animals seem to stick together in a herd.

Ah, yes — let's talk about why! Animals like zebras, gazelles, and antelopes are herbivores that eat mostly grass. Another way to say that these animals eat grass is that they **graze** (said this way: grāz). The savannah is a grassland, and there is usually plenty of grass available. This allows grazing animals to live and travel together in groups as they graze.

That makes sense. Are there any other benefits for the animals that live together in a herd?

There are! Powerful predators, like the lion, also live in the savannah. When an animal is alone, it cannot see in every direction to watch for predators. But when animals live together in a herd, there are many animals all on the lookout for predators. This helps to keep them all safe.

For example, if a zebra were all by itself, a lion would be able to easily sneak up on it. When there are many zebras all watching for predators together, though, it's much harder for the predator.

Yes. Being together in a group also means that the strong animals can help to protect the very young and old animals from predators. Living in a herd has many benefits for the animals in the savannah!

applyit Many different animals live in the savannah. Find each type of animal in the word search below!

Giraffe   Gazelle   Elephant   Zebra   Antelope   Meerkat   Leopard

Z	X	Y	T	U	K	L	M	D	N	G
E	L	E	P	H	A	N	T	R	B	I
B	M	E	E	R	K	A	T	A	V	R
R	C	A	P	A	R	I	E	P	C	A
A	N	T	E	L	O	P	E	O	X	F
Y	K	J	H	G	F	D	S	E	Z	F
J	P	K	Q	G	A	Z	E	L	L	E

You can learn more about meerkats in *God's Big Book of Animals*.

Hello, friend! I'm glad you're back for another science adventure. Ben has been learning all about some of the animals that live in the savannah, and I think he's ready to share with us today!

I am! There are so many animals we could talk about — let's start with zebras.

Ooh, zebras are one of my favorite animals! I've always thought that their stripes were a pretty design.

Speaking of stripes, if you looked quickly at several zebras, you might think that their stripe patterns were all the same. But if you began to look closely, you'd find that God created zebras to each have a unique pattern of stripes.

Really? That's like the way God created our fingerprints — no one has exactly the same fingerprint as someone else.

Isn't that amazing? But a zebra's stripes are more than just pretty or unique; they actually help to protect the animal from predators. When a herd of zebras are together, it can be difficult for predators to see each individual zebra because all the stripes blend together. This makes hunting much more difficult.

Zebras are an important part of the savannah. They have symbiotic relationships with a few different creatures. For example, you may find a zebra in the savannah with a bird called an oxpecker sitting on it. The oxpecker eats insects, like ticks, from the zebra.

That's mutualism, a type of symbiotic relationship! The oxpecker receives a meal, and the zebra gets rid of those pesky insects.

Right! In the savannah, you may also see herds of zebras and wildebeest (said this way: wĭl-dŭh-bēst) together. They have an interesting relationship because wildebeest only like to eat from short grass — but zebras don't really care what part of the grass they eat! A herd of zebras will eat the taller grass, and then the wildebeest will come behind them and eat the shorter part that they really like.

 The zebra's stripes can make it difficult for predators to pick out one zebra — especially when they are all moving together! How many zebras do you see in this picture?

Did their pattern of stripes make it easier or harder for you to count them?

We've been learning about some of the animals that live in the savannah lately. Are there any other creatures you can tell us about, Ben?

There are so many more creatures — I wish we had time to learn about all of them. Today, though, let's learn about the bird that is both the largest and fastest running bird in the world. The ostrich!

Ooh, this is going to be so much fun! Do you remember that ostrich at the zoo that kept following you around? It really liked you!

Yeah, I was worried he would escape and follow us home! The ostrich can grow to be up to 9 feet tall, which makes it the tallest bird alive in the world. A large ostrich can weigh over 300 pounds! While an ostrich cannot fly, it does have strong, powerful legs that allow it to run at speeds of around 40 miles per hour.

Wow, that is really fast! Being able to run that fast must help them be able to escape from a predator.

It does! Their powerful legs are also dangerous. An ostrich can kick with enough force to kill even a lion. That is one powerful kick!

In the African savannah, you may find ostriches and zebras living together.

Hmm, I think we're going to find another symbiotic relationship here!

You're right! The ostrich has a long neck and strong eyesight, which help it to see predators. But it isn't able to hear or smell very well. On the other hand, the zebra can hear and smell potential predators. But it can't see as well as the ostrich.

So together, they use their strengths to help each other. The zebra may smell a predator before the ostrich can see it. When the zebra alerts other zebras to the predator, it is also alerting the ostrich.

And when the ostrich sees a predator, as it alerts other ostriches, it's also alerting the zebras to danger. Together, the strengths of the zebra and ostrich help each other.

applyit How are the zebra and ostrich able to help each other?

_____

_____

_____

_____

_____

_____

_____

_____

DIGGING DEEPER The next time you're in the car, ask the driver to tell you when the car reaches a speed of 40 miles per hour. Imagine an ostrich running beside you at that same speed!

I've sure enjoyed learning about a few of the animals that live in the savannah. As we've been learning, I've also been thinking about how many herbivores live together in herds in this biome. In the savannah, a herd provides safety for the animal.

That's true! We've also seen how different animals live closely together because their different strengths benefit each other.

It reminds me of something I read in the Book of Ecclesiastes this week. Ecclesiastes was written by King Solomon, who was one of King David's sons. God gave Solomon a lot of wisdom and understanding. In Ecclesiastes 4:9–10, he wrote,

Two people are better than one. They can help each other in everything they do. Suppose either of them falls down. Then the one can help the other one up. But suppose a person falls down and doesn't have anyone to help them up. Then feel sorry for that person (NIrV)!

We can live and work together just as the zebra, wildebeest, and ostrich do. God gave each of us different talents and abilities — just like He did the animals. Our different talents and abilities help and benefit one another.

I'm really good at math, and sometimes I help Hannah with her math. Hannah is really good at writing, and she helps me think of creative stories to write.

We work together and help each other to grow.

And don't forget, we can also get big jobs done faster when we work together.

Remember when we needed to rake all those leaves up this fall? It would have taken me a long time all by myself. But together, we got it done in just an hour. I'm glad I have my family and friends to live and work together with!

Lions are powerful predators in the savannah. You can learn more about lions in *God's Big Book of Animals*.

Oh, good, you're back! Did you bring your Science Notebook? It's time to add a new page to it today!

I've got an idea — let's draw a zebra this week. I have a picture we can use for an example right here.

Great idea! I'm excited to draw the stripes on my zebra. And guess what? Just like real zebras, each of our zebras will be unique!

Here's what all of our zebras look like. I think Ben and Sam's turned out so cute! Have fun creating yours.

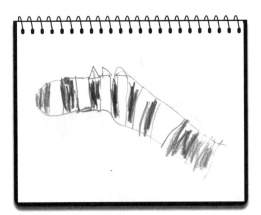

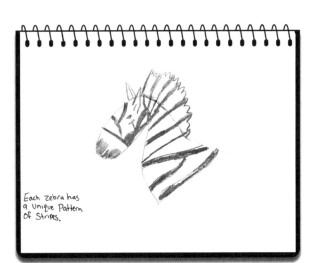

notebook

In your Science Notebook, write: **Each zebra has a unique pattern of stripes.**

Then, draw a picture of a zebra.

 **Hidden Treasure**

Learning about herds this week also reminded us that God gave us each different talents and abilities. We can use our talents and abilities to help one another. Copy Ecclesiastes 4:9 on the back of your Notebook page as a reminder.

Two people are better than one. They can help each other in everything they do (Ecclesiastes 4:9).

Grassland Biome Project

Day

I've had so much fun exploring the savannah with you over the last few weeks! Can you believe it's already time to create our model of the savannah biome? I've gathered up some of the supplies we'll need to get started today.

I have an idea for our model! There was a beautiful picture of a savannah sunset in one of the books I read recently. Can we paint a sunset as the background in our model biome?

I love that idea!

Okay — I have the picture right here that we can use for an example. See how the sky has beautiful shades of orange, yellow, and red?

Oh, that is beautiful! I love sunsets. We can begin by painting the colors in the sky. Let's get started!

Activity directions:

1. Spread out a tablecloth to protect the table.

2. Use orange acrylic paint to paint the inside of your shoebox. You'll want to paint the back, top, and sides orange. Then, rinse the paintbrush in the water and dry it on the paper towel.

3. Allow the paint to dry for a few minutes.

4. Paint a yellow sun on the back of the shoebox. Once you're done, rinse the paintbrush in the water and dry it on the paper towel.

5. If you'd like, you can also use shades of red and yellow to add more colors to the sunset.

6. Put the shoebox in a safe place to dry. We'll add more tomorrow!

7. Carefully rinse out your paintbrush.

Day

Our savannah sunset turned out so pretty! What should we add to our biome today?

Well, the picture we used to give us an idea for how to paint our biome also had a tree in it. We can paint a large acacia tree in the background of our biome today.

Great idea! Since the tree is in the shadows, we can use brown paint to paint the trunk, branches, and leaves.

Sounds good! Friend, if you'd like to paint your tree with green leaves, you're welcome to do that too. Be sure to have fun creating and painting the tree in your biome!

Activity directions:

1. Spread out a tablecloth to protect the table.

2. Paint an acacia tree in the background of your biome. You can use this acacia tree (below) as an example if you'd like!

3. Put the shoebox in a safe place to dry. We'll add more tomorrow!

4. Carefully rinse out your paintbrush.

materials needed

☐ Acrylic paint set

☐ Tablecloth to protect table

☐ Paintbrush

Our model of the savannah biome is looking good! Let's paint some grasses in the background of our box today.

That sounds like fun! Then, we can add the ground. I was thinking we could use some sand to add the ground — and I have an idea to make it look like a grassy field.

Okay! This is going to be interesting. I'll spread the tablecloth on the table so we can get started.

Activity directions:

materials needed

- [ ] Acrylic paint set
- [ ] Tablecloth to protect table
- [ ] Paintbrush
- [ ] Ziploc® bag
- [ ] Small bag of sand
- [ ] Green food coloring

1. Spread out a tablecloth to protect the table.

2. Paint patches of grass along the bottom of your model biome. You could use green, brown, or yellow paint for the grasses.

3. Carefully rinse out your paintbrush.

4. Pour most of your sand into the Ziploc® bag. Be sure to save about one handful of sand to add to the biome tomorrow.

5. Ask your teacher to add 10–15 drops of green food coloring to the sand in the bag.

6. Seal the Ziploc® bag. Then, shake and rub the sand through the bag so that the food coloring turns the sand green. You can ask your teacher to add more food coloring, if needed.

7. Once the paint is dry, carefully add the green sand to the bottom of your shoebox.

8. Put the shoebox in a safe place. We'll add more tomorrow!

Day

We're almost done creating our model savannah biome! We have just a few more things to add to it now.

It's exciting to see it come together, isn't it? Let's add a watering hole to the biome today. We can use more sand to create the watering hole for the animals we'll add tomorrow!

Activity directions:

1. Pour the leftover sand from day 3 into a Ziploc® bag.

2. Ask your teacher to add 10–15 drops of blue food coloring to the sand in the bag.

3. Seal the Ziploc® bag. Then, shake and rub the sand through the bag so that the food coloring turns the sand blue. You can ask your teacher to add more food coloring, if needed.

4. Decide where you would like the watering hole to be in your biome. Carefully use the spoon to scoop the sand out of the bag and add it to your biome.

5. Put the shoebox in a safe place. We'll add more tomorrow!

materials needed

- ☐ Tablecloth to protect table
- ☐ Ziploc® bag
- ☐ Leftover sand from day 3
- ☐ Blue food coloring
- ☐ Spoon

Today is the day! We're all ready to finish up our savannah biome by adding some animals to it. I have some lions, a zebra, giraffe, and an elephant here and ready to go!

What are we waiting for? Let's finish our savannah biome!

We have some small, model animals that we are going to put into our biome. If you don't have any, you can also use playdough to create some or ask your teacher to help you find and print some pictures you can use.

Activity directions:

1. Add the small animals to your savannah biome model.

2. Share your biome with your family. Be sure to tell them what you've learned about the savannah and God's design in this biome.

Bonus! Take a picture of your savannah biome and ask your teacher to help you print it out. Then tape or glue the picture on the next page in your Science Notebook. Write **My Savannah Biome** at the top of the page.

The Image of God

Day

Welcome back, friend! Can you believe we've explored four of the earth's biomes together in our adventures this year?

It was so much fun learning about the boreal forest, temperate deciduous forest, tropical rainforest, and the savannah grassland. I've loved finding God's design, care, and wisdom in different parts of creation.

Me too. We've also been able to discover many of the relationships God placed in creation. There is one relationship I'm still wondering about, though. What is our relationship with creation as human beings?

Ah, that is a great question, Ben! Where do you think we should start in order to answer it?

Hmm, we should definitely start with the Bible!

Exactly right! Let's read Genesis 1:27–28 together to get started:

So God created human beings in his own likeness. He created them to be like himself. He created them as male and female. God blessed them. He said to them, "Have children so that there will be many of you. Fill the earth and bring it under your control. Rule over the fish in the seas and the birds in the sky. Rule over every living creature that moves along the ground" (NIrV).

Wait, what does it mean to be created in the likeness of God? Does that mean we look like God does?

Good question! No, to be made in God's likeness doesn't mean that we look like Him. Instead, it means that we reflect the character and attributes of God. Another way to say that we've been made in the likeness of God is that we are made in His image.

Character is a word that means the features or traits of something, and an attribute means a quality of something. We'll dig deeper into what it means to be created in the image of God tomorrow — I hear Mom calling us for lunch now!

 **applyit** Copy Genesis 1:27:

So God created human beings in his own likeness. He created them to be like himself. He created them as male and female.

I'm excited to continue our conversation today! Yesterday, we read Genesis 1:27–28 together, and we learned that God created human beings in His image. Hannah, you mentioned that being made in God's image means that we reflect His character and attributes. Can you tell us more about what that means?

Sure! First, let's think about it like this: Dad likes to tell silly, unexpected jokes. That is part of his character, or an attribute, of who Dad is. Ben, you are Dad's son, and you also like to tell silly, unexpected jokes! You and Dad share a similar sense of humor. This is one way you reflect what Dad is like. You don't look exactly like Dad, but you reflect part of who he is.

Ah, okay, that makes sense.

We learn about God's character and attributes in the Bible. In 1 John 4:8, we learn that God is love, and Deuteronomy 32:4 tells us that God is just. We see God's grace, compassion, and mercy throughout the Bible. When we study creation, we also see that God is creative and organized.

God created humans to reflect His character and attributes. For example, when we love each other, we're also showing others God's loving character. We're reflecting God's love.

Wait, people aren't always loving, Hannah. Sometimes people aren't merciful either. I've seen people be very mean to each other. Sometimes I've even been very mean to someone else.

You're right, Ben. Remember, in the beginning, God created human beings in His image. Before sin, people would have reflected the image of God perfectly. But then sin entered and stained the perfect image of God in us.

Human beings still bear the image of God — but it is imperfect and broken now. When we are unloving, unjust, unmerciful, unkind, and ungracious, we reflect the image of sin rather than the image of God. Hmm, I have an idea for an activity to help us understand how sin stained the original creation.

Activity directions:

materials needed

☐ Tablecloth

☐ White paper

☐ Washable paint

☐ Paintbrush

1. Spread out a tablecloth to protect the table.

2. Place the piece of paper on the table. The paper is perfect and pure; it's an example of the way humans would have reflected the image of God before sin.

3. Ask your teacher to help you spread paint on your hands.

4. Now, try to pick up the piece of paper with your hands. What happens? The paint is an example of sin, and it has stained the paper — the same way sin stained God's perfect creation.

5. Next, try to rub off the paint from the paper with your hands. What happens? Now there is even more paint smeared on the paper!

6. Just as the paper is now stained by the paint, God's perfect creation was also stained by sin. You weren't able to remove the paint from the paper, just as we are not able to save ourselves from sin. We'll be talking more about that soon!

Thanks for telling us more about what it means to be made in the image of God, Hannah! Are there any other ways human beings reflect God's image?

There sure are! When we explore creation, we see God's creativity in the colors of the scarlet macaw, the suction cup feet of the red-eyed tree frog, and so much more. God gave human beings the ability to be creative as well through language, art, and the things we create.

In the Bible, we also see that God is sovereign; He has rule and authority over all things. While humans do not have rule over all things as God does, God did give humans rule over the earth in Genesis. We're going to be talking more about what that means soon!

I'm looking forward to that. In the meantime, I have another question. I was reading a book about monkeys the other day. In the book, it said that we organize monkeys as primates (said this way: prī-māts).

Ah, yes. As we've seen in our science adventures, scientists organize plants, animals, and birds into different categories or groups. Monkeys, apes, and lemurs are organized as primates.

But the book also said that humans are organized as primates too. Does that mean that animals, like monkeys, were also made in the image of God?

Great question, Ben. I'm glad you asked. No, in Genesis we read that only human beings were created to be in the image of God. God created both animals and people — but God only created people in His image. That makes human beings different from the animals.

Scientists work to organize the things we see on the earth — but they don't always organize creation by starting with the Bible. Scientists organize humans and monkeys together because we see similar designs in them both.

Like the way humans and monkeys have eyes on the front of their faces!

Yes, but similar designs do not mean that humans are animals too. Sometimes we do see similar designs between humans and animals because God created them both — but God only created humans in His image. Being made in God's image — to reflect His character and attributes — is what makes people different from the animals.

apply it — Why are human beings different from the animals?

I'm glad we were able to spend some time learning how God created people in His image this week! I'm also excited to learn more about what it means to rule over the earth. In the meantime, though, I've been thinking about how sin stained and broke the perfect image of God in us.

In our activity the other day, we saw there wasn't a way for us to remove the stain of paint from the paper. No matter what we did, it just made it worse!

Very true. Just like we saw in our activity, there isn't a way that we can save ourselves from sin or remove its stain all by ourselves. But that's not the end of the story. In Isaiah 1:18, we read,

"Come now, let us settle the matter," says the LORD. "Though your sins are like scarlet, they shall be as white as snow; though they are red as crimson, they shall be like wool."

When Jesus died on the cross, He paid the price for our sin. Only He is able to wash the stain of sin so that we can have a relationship with God again. Romans 3:23–24 tells us,

Everyone has sinned. No one measures up to God's glory. The free gift of God's grace makes us right with him. Christ Jesus paid the price to set us free (NIrV).

And that's not all! When we've trusted in Jesus to redeem — to save us — from sin, we also begin to grow more like Him. We read in Colossians 3:10 that

You have started living a new life. Your knowledge of how that life should have the Creator's likeness is being made new (NIrV).

As we read our Bible and pray, we learn more and more about how God wants us to live our lives. Day by day, when we submit our lives to God's instructions, our lives begin to look more and more like the life Jesus lived.

Wow! So as we follow Jesus, He begins to remove the image of sin from our lives and restore the image of God.

It doesn't mean that we will be perfect — we will still make sinful mistakes while we live on the earth. But when we make mistakes, we can ask for God's forgiveness. Then, we can continue submitting our lives to Him, and He will continue to make us new in His image.

Day

It's time to add another page to our Science Notebook today!

Yay! Let's draw a picture of ourselves this week, since we've been learning about how God made people in His image.

That sounds like fun! I can't wait to see how our pictures turn out.

Ta-da! Here is what all of our Notebooks look like. We're excited to see yours — don't forget to have fun!

God made human beings in His image.

God made human beings in His image.

In your Science Notebook, write: **God made human beings in His image.**

Then, draw a picture of yourself.

This week we learned that human beings were created in the image of God. Copy Genesis 1:27 on the back of your Notebook page as a reminder.

So God created human beings in his own likeness. He created them to be like himself. He created them as male and female (Genesis 1:27).

Stewardship

Day

Hello, friend! Now that we've learned about how human beings are created in the image of God, it's time to dig deeper and learn more about our relationship with creation. Let's start by reading Genesis 1:28 together,

God blessed them. He said to them, "Have children so that there will be many of you. Fill the earth and bring it under your control. Rule over the fish in the seas and the birds in the sky. Rule over every living creature that moves along the ground" (NIrV).

Hmm, in that verse God told Adam and Eve to bring the earth under their control, to rule over the fish, birds, and every living creature.

Another way we can say this is that God gave human beings dominion over the earth. **Dominion** (said this way: dŭh-mĭn-yŭhn) means the power to rule over something.

Okay, does having dominion over the earth mean that we are free to do whatever we want with it?

Great question, Ben! A king has control, power, and dominion over his kingdom, just as we were given over creation. Let me tell you a story about two kings to help answer your question.

The first king ruled over a large land. He had power and control over all the creatures and people who lived in his kingdom — but he did not care for them. He took from the people and made them serve him. He treated the animals cruelly, forcing them to work hard for little food. He took what he wanted from the land and did not care for it. Soon, the beautiful plants began to die, and thorns and thistles took their place.

The second king also ruled over a large land. He had power and control over all the creatures and people who lived in his kingdom — and he cared for them. He gave to the people and made sure their needs were met. Though the animals also worked for him, he treated them kindly. His animals always had plenty of food and care. He tended to the plants and trees in his kingdom. Beautiful gardens grew there and provided delicious food for all to enjoy.

Dad is calling us for dinner, so we'll have to continue talking about dominion tomorrow. In the meantime, think about which kingdom you would rather live in.

applyit Would you rather live in the first kingdom or the second kingdom?

Why?

I'm excited to continue learning about dominion today! Hannah, I've been thinking about the kingdoms you told us about yesterday. I would rather live in the second one because that king took care of his kingdom.

I agree! Both kings had the same power and authority over their kingdoms. But the first king did whatever he wanted — and everything suffered as a result. The second king used his power and authority for the good of his kingdom.

Ah, I get it! God gave us dominion to rule over the earth — but we need to use our authority wisely for the good of creation.

Right! Dominion doesn't mean that we do whatever we want, but that we care for creation the same way God cares for us. We want to tend to God's creation and manage it wisely — to be good stewards. The word steward means to manage, look after, and care for something that belongs to someone else.

God created the earth and all that is in it. Creation belongs to God — but He has given it to us to manage, to steward. We want to be good stewards of what He has placed in our care.

What are some ways people can be good stewards of God's creation, Hannah?

One important way is that we learn all we can about how God designed creation to work. For example, we can study plants or animals to learn more about what they need. This helps us to care for them better. As we study and learn, there are times we notice something isn't quite right.

Like when the wolves disappeared from Yellowstone National Park!

When we notice something isn't quite right in creation, we can work to help fix it. Sometimes that might mean we help bring a creature or plant back to an environment. Other times, we may find a creature or plant where it really doesn't belong — it has invaded an environment and is causing harm. When that happens, we can help to remove it. We'll talk more about other ways we can be good stewards tomorrow.

applyit What does the word steward mean?

Let's continue talking about stewardship today! As we've seen throughout our adventures, God provided many resources in creation through plants, animals, water, land, trees, energy, and more. We can use these resources wisely to benefit creation.

For example, water is a resource that we all need. We want to maintain clean water to drink and play in. To do this, we can use our creativity to find ways to filter dirty water. We can also work to keep ponds, lakes, rivers, and oceans clean.

One important way we do that is by making sure our garbage is taken care of. When there is garbage where it doesn't belong, we call it litter. Litter can harm the people, plants, animals, birds, and insects that live in an area.

Another way we can use resources wisely is to be careful not to waste water, food, and the energy that powers our home. We can turn off the faucet when we're done using water. We can also turn off lights or other things that are powered by electricity once we're done using them.

We've also noticed during our adventures together that God designed creation to recycle and reuse all different things so that nothing is wasted. That reminds me of the movie we watched on how we can recycle plastic, glass, and metal to be made into something new!

I'm glad you mentioned that! Recycling allows things like plastic, glass, and metal containers to be made into something new. We can help sort our containers at home so that they can be recycled. We can also recycle things like clothing we've outgrown or toys we no longer play with by giving them to someone else who can use them. These are great ways to keep from being wasteful!

We can also be good stewards of creation by taking care of the animals around us in our home or environment.

Like our cat Bell and the fish in our fish tank! We also help care for the beautiful birds in our yard by placing bird feeders out in the winter when food is harder for them to find.

We love animals and birds; they make us smile and laugh. We want to take good care of them because God created animals too.

applyit Can you think of any ways you can be a good steward of God's creation?

DIGGING DEEPER Animal rescues care for animals that are sick, injured, or abandoned. Some animal rescues take care of wild animals, while others take care of cats and dogs. Ask your teacher to help you find out if there is an animal rescue in your area. What kind of animals do they care for? What do you think it would be like to work at an animal rescue?

Day

I've had fun exploring good stewardship this week! But Hannah, I have a question. Creation is so big and we're just kids — how can we start to care for and manage creation wisely?

Good question! The best way to start is by developing good habits in taking care of the things God has already given us.

Like our home, our rooms, toys, pets, and clothes?

Right! It reminds me of Luke 16:10:

Whoever can be trusted with very little can also be trusted with much, and whoever is dishonest with very little will also be dishonest with much.

If we don't know how to care for the small things God has given us, we won't be able to care for larger things in God's creation either. We can begin by being careful to not waste the food, energy, water, and other resources we have available.

Another way we can learn to be good stewards as kids is to take care of the land around us. Wherever we live, we can make sure we take care of our garbage to help keep the land around us clean. We can also help to care for the land around our homes or ask our parents to help us find ways to help care for the land in our community.

Like the neighborhood cleanup day we helped with last spring! We helped our neighbors clean up litter from the side of the road. We also helped clean up the dead twigs and branches that had fallen from the trees over the winter.

I also like to help our neighbor pull the weeds out of her garden. These are all good ways we can start learning how to be good stewards of God's creation. I think Mom and Dad will have more ideas for us too — let's be sure to ask them tonight at dinner.

Ask your family about ways you can be a good steward of God's creation. You can talk about ways you already care for God's creation, and maybe develop some new ideas as well!

Day

We sure learned a lot this week. It was fun talking about good stewardship with you!

You know what time it is now! Let's add a new page to our Science Notebook.

What should we draw this week, Ben?

Let's draw a crown to remind us that we have been given rule over the earth, and like the second king in the story, we want to be wise stewards of what we've been given.

Great idea! Here is a picture of a crown that we can use to give us an idea for how to draw it. We can draw gems on our crowns, and even add glitter if we'd like!

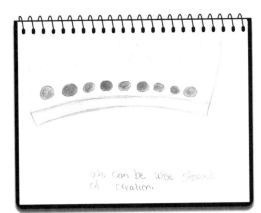

Here's what each of our crowns look like — have fun creating yours!

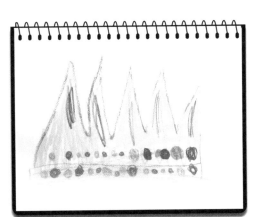

notebook In your Science Notebook, write: **We can be wise stewards of creation.**

Then, draw a picture of a crown.

 We can be good stewards by caring for the things God has already given us. As we care for the small things, we're also learning how to care for bigger things. Copy Luke 16:10 on the back of your Notebook page as a reminder.

Whoever can be trusted with very little can also be trusted with much, and whoever is dishonest with very little will also be dishonest with much (Luke 16:10).

Review

Day

Hello, friend! We've reached our last science adventure together for now. Can you believe it? We've explored so much of God's creation this year!

It has been a lot of fun — and I'm looking forward to continuing to explore God's creation as I get older.

I have an idea; let's take a look back at everything we learned about this year. Go get your Science Notebook so we can look through all of our drawings together!

Okay! We can start with the very first page — remember those squirrels we drew? We learned about habitats, ecosystems, and biomes that first week. We also read Proverbs 2:3–5 together:

Indeed, if you call out for insight and cry aloud for understanding, and if you look for it as for silver and search for it as for hidden treasure, then you will understand the fear of the LORD and find the knowledge of God.

We learned that as we look for and document God's design in creation, we'll also learn more about God. It's like finding a hidden treasure! Habitats reminded us that God is our dwelling place and that we can trust Him.

A habitat is the natural environment a plant or animal lives in.

Let's look at the next drawing in our Notebook. We learned about the climate of the boreal forest, swamps, and permafrost next. Swamps reminded us that unforgiveness can create a stinky mess inside our hearts.

We learned that we can show mercy, kindness, and forgiveness to others because we know that God has also forgiven us. Ooh, look at the next page in our Notebook! We learned about coniferous trees and how God designed them to thrive even during cold winters. Do you remember our hidden treasure that week, Ben?

I do! Life isn't always easy, but God cares for us during hard times. Next, we learned about the lodgepole pine tree. Turn to that page in your Notebook. We discovered how God created them with two types of pinecones. One type scatters the seeds once they're ready, and the other kind scatters the seeds after a forest fire. We also talked about Joseph's life in the Bible. Forest fires reminded us that God works all things together for the good of those who love Him.

applyit What part of the boreal forest biome did you enjoy exploring the most?

Day

Isn't it fun to look back through our Science Notebook and see all the things we've learned about this year? After the lodgepole pine, we began to learn about the food chain. Turn to the food chain drawing in your Notebook. The food chain shows us how energy moves through creation. It also reminds us that God's original, perfect creation was broken by sin. We see the sad effects of sin through the food chain.

Then, we talked more about the food chain, predators, the trophic pyramid, and apex predators. We got to draw a picture of a wolf that week. Can you find your wolf in the Notebook? Our hidden treasure in that lesson was one of my favorites. We learned from Isaiah 11:6 that someday, God will restore creation and the wolf will no longer be an apex predator.

The wolf is an apex Predator.

We all look forward to that day! Turn to the next page — remember the beavers we all drew? We learned about the food web as we explored Yellowstone National Park. We learned how wolves disappeared from the park and how that affected so many other creatures.

It was amazing! We saw how even in the death and destruction sin brought to the world, God designed creation so that it could maintain balance. This allows so many diverse species of birds, plants, and animals to live together in an ecosystem.

Look at the next page. We also learned how wolves returned to the park and how balance began to be restored. We saw how each relationship within creation, big or small, proclaims the glory, majesty, and incredible wisdom of God. And then it was time to create our boreal forest shoebox model. That was so much fun!

Up next we began to explore the temperate deciduous forest — we learned about the climate of that biome, species, and the opossum.

Oh, I remember! Turn to the opossum drawing. Opossums pretend they are dead so that they can stay safe from danger and continue living. That reminded us of Romans 6:11 and how we also die to sin so that we can live alive in Jesus: *"In the same way, count yourselves dead to sin but alive to God in Christ Jesus."* Turn to the next page in the Notebook — we learned all about deciduous trees after that!

The Opossum lives in the temperate deciduous forest.

We also talked about seasons, which reminded us that there is a time for everything in our lives. We can trust God with the season we are in right now.

applyit What part of the temperate deciduous forest biome did you enjoy exploring the most?

I'm so glad we created our Science Notebooks this year. I love looking back to see all the things we learned about creation and about God. The next page in our Notebook shows deciduous trees and the forest canopy. Just as the forest canopy protects the forest, we learned how God is our strength and our shield — our protector.

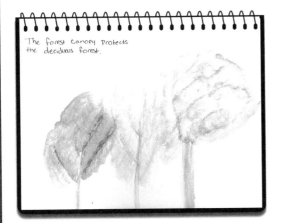

The forest canopy protects the deciduous forest.

We began to explore under the forest canopy next. Turn to that page in your Notebook! We learned about trees and shrubs, as well as how the different parts of a tree all work together. It reminded us of how God has given each of us different gifts and abilities.

The forest floor was next as we continued exploring the layers of the forest. Can you find that page in your Notebook? We learned about how leaf litter provides nutrients all through the year. The layers of the forest also reminded us that suffering, perseverance, character, and hope layer upon each other and cause us to grow. As we grow, our lives look more like Christ.

Leaf litter provides nutrients for the forest during the year.

Turn to the next page. We learned about decomposition and earthworms in the following lesson. Decomposers reminded us that only God can bring us from death to life. It is His power that frees us from sin.

Now, turn to your drawing of lichens. We found a hidden treasure in that lesson too. Lichens remind us that relationships are important — we can impact others for good or for bad.

We learned about symbiotic relationships next, and we drew pictures of flowers and bees. We also learned about parasites — and it reminded us that we can serve others and show them God's love rather than be selfish. After that, we created our temperate deciduous forest biome!

Mutualism is a symbiotic relationship where two organisms receive a benefit

The tropical rainforest biome is found near the equator.

Then we were off to explore the tropical rainforest; that was one of my favorite biomes! In our first lesson, we explored the climate and how the rainforest is found near the equator. Can you find that drawing in your Notebook? When we learned about the large amount of rain this biome receives, it reminded us that God supplies the earth with rain. Then it was time to explore the layers of the rainforest.

We started with the emergent layer and explored pollinating bats, the kapok tree, and buttress roots. Can you find your bat drawing? Learning about the buttress roots of the kapok tree also reminded us that a firm foundation is very important. God is the only firm foundation we can build our lives upon.

applyit   What part of the tropical rainforest biome did you enjoy exploring the most?

Do you have your Science Notebook with you? Let's keep looking through our drawings! We learned about the rainforest canopy next. It was really interesting to explore epiphytes. Turn to your epiphyte drawing in your Notebook.

The Scarlet macaw lives in the rainforest.

We also learned about the poison dart frog that week, and it reminded us that words can be like poison to others. Turn to the next page in your Notebook — we learned about macaws and the harpy eagle in the following lesson. Matthew 10:31 reminded us that God cares for even the birds. We don't have to be afraid because God cares much more for us.

We learned about the sloth in the next lesson — let's see your sloth drawing! We saw how the sloth uses its energy wisely, which reminded us that we can use our talents and abilities wisely too. We serve Jesus in all that we do, and we can always do our very best.

Turn to the next page in your Notebook, the howler monkey! Monkeys reminded us that God is always trustworthy, faithful, and working things out to show His glory in our lives.

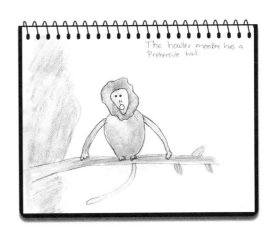

The howler monkey has a prehensile tail.

After that it was time to explore the understory, and we learned about predators there. We saw that the boa constrictor and jaguar wait to surprise their prey. Sometimes, it can feel like temptation surprises us too. But 1 Corinthians 10:13 reminds us that God is faithful and He doesn't leave us alone when we are tempted. We can ask for His help to make the right choice.

Finally, we explored the forest floor and learned about leaf-cutter ants. They work hard, and it is a reminder that we can also work diligently in whatever job we are given to do. After that, it was time to create our rainforest biome model!

Leaf-cutter ants gather leaves to grow fungus on.

Tropical grasslands are called Savannas.

Turn to the next page in your Notebook where we began our exploration of the grassland! We learned about temperate and tropical grasslands. We talked about the dry season, which reminded us that we must seek God, just as we would seek water in a dry land. Then, we learned more about grass, and that was so interesting!

Our hidden treasure that week was Isaiah 40:8, *"The grass withers and the flowers fall, but the word of our God endures forever."*

Then, we explored acacia trees — turn to that drawing. Their thorns reminded us that thorns were part of the consequences for sin and that Jesus wore a crown of thorns when He paid the price of sin for us.

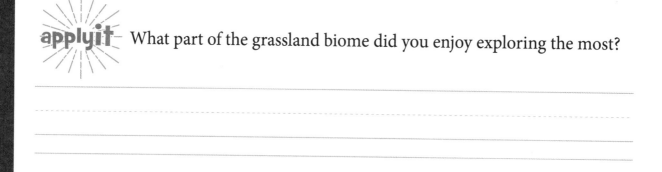

applyit What part of the grassland biome did you enjoy exploring the most?

We're almost done looking back through the pages in our Science Notebooks! Turn to your elephant drawing; we learned about those next! We saw all the ways elephants help the savannah. It reminded us that we can be sure to speak helpful words that build others up.

The African elephant is a keystone species.

Then, Ben shared about the zebra and savannah herds. The way different animals live together to benefit one another reminded us that we can use our talents and abilities to help others too. We made our savannah biome after that!

We also learned that God created human beings in His image — and we explored what it means to be made in the image of God. It was fun to draw a picture of ourselves! After that, it was time to explore ways we can be good stewards of what God has given us and the earth He created.

God made human beings in His image.

Wow, we learned about so much this year, and we discovered God's design all over creation!

That is my favorite part of studying science. Science is a tool God has given us to explore His creation and to learn more about Him. It also teaches us more about our relationship with Him. As we all continue growing up, we're going to get to study so many other branches of science like biology, chemistry, physics, and more!

The more we learn and explore, the more we can see God's wisdom, majesty, mercy, care, and design in His creation. Even though this science adventure is coming to a close, we can each continue to look for God's design in whatever part of science we are exploring — and we'll find it!

Indeed. Hey, we have one more page to add to our Science Notebook!

We do! Let's draw a magnifying glass today. A magnifying glass helps us to take a closer look at something. We can draw one as a reminder that no matter what part of science we study in the future, we can look closely for God's design. When we do, we will discover His wisdom, creativity, majesty, mercy, care, and design.

Here is a picture we can use for an example.

Here's what our magnifying glasses look like! Don't forget to share your drawing with someone else and tell them all about what you've learned this year. Then, have fun continuing to explore science!

notebook

In your Science Notebook, write: **We can look for God's design in every branch of science.**

Then draw a picture of a magnifying glass.

Science reveals God's design, wisdom, creativity, majesty, mercy, and care. It reminds us that God is worthy to receive glory, praise, honor, and power. Copy Revelation 4:11 on the back of your Notebook page as a reminder.

You are worthy, our Lord and God, to receive glory and honor and power, for you created all things, and by your will they were created and have their being (Revelation 4:11).

BONUS Activities

These activities and ideas can be used to enhance your student's learning experience as they complete *Adventures on Planet Earth*.

1. Plan a trip to a zoo, aquarium, aviary, or botanical gardens. Plants and wildlife are often grouped by biome or region of the world. See if you can identify the different biomes plants or creatures would live in.

2. Choose a biome and purchase a plant that would grow there. This could be a houseplant or something you can add to your garden. Here are some plant ideas:

   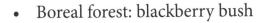

   - Boreal forest: blackberry bush

   - Deciduous forest: fern, violets

   - Tropical rainforest: orchid, snake plant

   - Grassland: grasses, wildflowers

   Note: some plants may be toxic for children or pets to ingest.

3. Depending on your location and the season, plant a small garden and teach your student how to care for the plants.

4. Find a documentary that shows how material such as plastic and glass is recycled. If you have a local recycling center, they may also offer a tour.

5. See if you have a wildlife rescue and rehabilitation center in your area. They may offer a tour or provide ways your family could help.

6. Plan a yard or neighborhood cleanup day.

7. Depending on your location and the season, plan a trip to a maple sugar house shortly before or after the student completes week 12.

8. Learn to identify common types of trees or plants found in your area.

9. Purchase a bird identification guide then set up a bird feeder in your yard. Learn to identify the birds in your area.

10. What wildlife is common in your area? Pick an animal to learn more about.

11. If you live close to a state or national park, plan a trip. Research the biome and some plants and animals that live in the park.

12. Plant a tree.

13. Answers TV features shows such as *Hide & Seek with Peter Schriemer* and *Out and About with Buddy Davis* that your student may enjoy. Find more at answers.tv.

14. Visit the Ark Encounter or the Creation Museum. Discuss what the world was like after creation before sin and death. Discuss changes to the earth after the Flood.

Basic Phonics Review

Phonetic pronunciations are included throughout this book. Your student may review the vowel symbols and pronunciation using this chart.

Vowel	As In	Vowel	As In	Vowel	As In
ă	dad	ĕ	men	ŏ	not
ā	cape	ē	be	ō	bone
å	far	ĭ	sit	ŭ	sun
		ī	like	ū	use

Glossary

A

Acidic (said this way: ĕh-sĭ-dĭk): high in acid.

Adapt (said this way: ŭh-dăpt): to adjust or change for certain conditions or a particular environment.

Amphibians (said this way: ăm-fĭb-ē-ĕns): amphibians are animals like frogs, toads, and salamanders.

Annually (said this way: ăn-yoo-ŭh-lē): each year.

Apex predator (said this way: āpĕx prĕ-dŭh-ter): a predator that is at the very top of the food chain. Apex predators do not have a natural predator.

B

Biome (bī-ōm): a very large habitat that contains many of the same types of plants and animals. A biome can be home to many ecosystems, such as a pond and a forest.

Buttress roots (said this way: bŭh-trĭs): the bottom of a tree trunk that fans out in wide, triangle shapes. Buttress roots give a tree a stable foundation and also help to draw nutrients into the tree.

C

Cambium (said this way: căm-bē-ŭm): a layer within a tree trunk. The cambium creates cells that cause the tree to grow.

Camouflage (said this way: kă-mŭh-flåzh): a way to stay hidden in an environment.

Carnivore (said this way: kår-nĕ-vōr): a consumer that only eats other fish or animals.

Chlorophyll (said this way: klōr-ō-fĭll): chlorophyll is found inside leaves and needles. It is what causes them to have a green color.

Climate (said this way: klī-mĕt): the usual, or typical, amount of rain, snow, cloud cover, and sunlight an environment will experience during a year.

Commensalism (said this way: kŭh-mĕn-sŭh-lĭz-ŭhm): a relationship between two organisms — but only one organism receives a benefit. The other organism is not harmed by the relationship.

Compound (said this way: kŏm-pŏwnd): means made of two or more parts.

Conifers (said this way: kȧ-nĭh-furs): trees that have needles on their branches instead of leaves. The needles usually do not turn brown or fall off during the winter — that is why we also call them "evergreen" trees because most conifer trees stay green throughout the whole year.

Consumer (said this way: kŭn-soo-mer): a consumer needs to consume, or eat, food from a plant or animal. It cannot make its own food like a plant.

Continent (said this way: kŏn-tĕ-nĕnt): a large area of land on the earth. The continents are Africa, Asia, Antarctica, Europe, Australia, North America, and South America.

D

Debris (said this way: dĕ-brē): the remains of something old, fallen, or broken.

Deciduous (said this way: dĭh-sĭj-ū-ŭs): trees that have leaves that fall off the tree before winter.

Decomposition (said this way: dē-cŏm-pō-zĭ-shŭn): the process in which dead plants and animals break back down into the soil.

Digestion (said this way: dī-jĕs-chĕn): the process our bodies use to break the food we eat down into nutrients we can absorb and energy we can use.

Diverse (said this way: dī-verse): a lot of variety or different kinds.

Dormant (said this way: dōr-mĕnt): resting, not active or growing.

Drought (said this way: drŏwt): a long period of time without rain.

E

Ecology (said this way: ĭh-cȧll-ō-jē): the study of the environment plants and animals live in, as well as the relationships between living and non-living things.

Ecosystem (said this way: ē-cō-sĭs-tŭm): all of the living and non-living things that are together in a place.

Efficiently (said this way: ĭh-fĭsh-ŭhnt-lē): done in the best way, without wasting anything.

Energy (said this way: ĕn-er-jēē): allows work to be done.

Environment (said this way: ĕn-vī-rŭn-mĕnt): the place a person, plant, or animal lives.

Enzyme (said this way: ĕn-zīm): a substance that digests or breaks down another substance.

Epiphyte (said this way: ĕp-ŭh-fīte): a type of plant that grows on top of other plants.

F

Female (said this way: fē-māl): a girl or woman.

Food chain: the links between plants and animals as they eat.

G

Glossary (said this way: glŏss-ŭh-rē): a tool that lists words and their meanings. It's usually found in the back of a book and the words are listed in alphabetical order.

Graze (said this way: grāz): to eat grass.

H

Habitat (said this way: hăb-ĭ-tăt): the natural environment a plant or animal lives in.

Herbivore (said this way: her-bĭh-vōr): a consumer that only eats plants.

Herd (said this way: hurd): a large group of the same type of animal.

Hyphae (said this way: hī-fŭh): grown by fungi. Hyphae are kind of like roots that branch out and attach to the material the fungus will digest.

K

Keystone species (said this way: kēē-stōne spē-shēz): a type of animal that the ecosystem depends upon. If a keystone species goes away, the ecosystem changes in ways we'll notice over time.

Kind (said this way: kīnd): a family group of animals, such as the bear kind.

L

Larva (said this way: lår-vŭh): baby insects.

M

Male (said this way: māl): a boy or man.

Mammal (said this way: măm-ŭhl): a type of creature that has a body with hair, feed their babies with milk, and has a spine.

Midrib (said this way: mĭd-rĭb): the large vein that runs through the middle of the leaf.

Mutualism (said this way: myoo-choo-ŭh-lĭz-ŭhm): a relationship in which two organisms receive a benefit from each other.

N

Nocturnal (said this way: nŏc-ter-nl): a creature that sleeps during the day and is active at night.

Nutrient (said this way: new-trēē-ĕnt): a substance that plants, animals, and people need to grow and live.

O

Omnivore (said this way: åm-nĭh-vōr): a consumer that eats both plants and other creatures.

Organism (said this way: ōr-guh-nĭz-ŭm): a living thing like a person, animal, plant, or even fungus.

P

Parasite (said this way: pair-ŭh-sīt): an organism that lives inside or on a different organism and receives nutrients from it.

Parasitism (said this way: pair-ŭh-sĕh-tĭzm): a relationship in which a parasite lives on a host.

Permafrost (said this way: per-mŭh-frŏst): ground that is frozen all the time, or permanently.

Petiole (said this way: pĕt-ē-ōhl): attaches a leaf to the branch.

Phloem (said this way: flō-ĕm): carries nutrients through the tree.

Photosynthesis (said this way: fō-tō-sĭn-the-sĭs): the process plants use to convert sunlight and carbon dioxide gas from the air into sugar that the plant uses and oxygen that we can breathe.

Pollinators (said this way: pŏl-ĭn-āt-ōrs): bees, butterflies, hummingbirds, bats, and other insects that pollinate flowers.

Pollution (said this way: pŭh-loo-shŭn): something harmful that has been released, or something that has contaminated something else.

Predator (said this way: prĕ-dŭh-ter): a consumer that kills and eats another creature.

Prey (said this way: prāy): animals that are killed and eaten by predators.

Primary consumers: only eat plants; they are herbivores. Many types of animals and insects are primary consumers.

Producers (said this way prō-doo-sers): plants that produce their own food through photosynthesis using energy from the sun.

R

Raptors (said this way: răp-ters): predator birds; they are carnivores.

Reptile (said this way: rĕ-tīl): an animal that crawls on its belly or has small legs. Reptiles are also cold-blooded. This means their bodies rely on the sun and the air around them to keep their bodies warm.

S

Secondary consumers: omnivores and carnivores that can be the prey of an apex predator.

Species (said this way: spē-shēēz): a kind of animal, bird, plant, or insect. Some examples of animal species would be gorillas, lions, dogs, squirrels, and raccoons.

Stewardship (said this way: stew-erd-shĭp): to manage, look after, and care for something that belongs to someone else.

Symbiotic relationship (said this way: sĭm-bē-ŏt-ĭk): organisms that live together in a close relationship.

T

Taproot (said this way: tăp-root): a long root that grows deep into the soil. Smaller roots may branch off of the taproot.

Temperate (said this way: tĕm-per-ĭt): mild or not extreme.

V

Vegetation (said this way: vĕ-jĕ-tā-shĕn): plant and tree life.

Venomous (said this way: vĕn-ŭh-mŭhs): a creature that possesses venom. Venom is a special type of poison some creatures can inject through a bite or a sting.

Vocabulary (said this way: vō-căb-ū-lĕh-rē): all the words that you know.

X

Xylem (said this way: zī-lŭhm): a layer of a tree that transports water through the tree.

Answer Keys

Page 24

Habitat – A natural environment that a plant or animal lives in.

Ecosystem – All of the living and non-living things that are together in a place.

Biome – A very large habitat that contains many of the same types of plants and animals.

Page 40

Page 52

needles

Page 56

Q	X	C	O	N	I	F	E	R	K	X
M	P	W	C	V	N	I	M	E	J	B
E	F	O	R	Q	P	R	T	S	L	F
R	L	D	J	F	G	E	H	I	B	I
C	K	P	I	N	E	C	O	N	E	R
Y	E	L	L	O	W	S	T	O	N	E

Page 62

2   4   1   3

Pages 65–66

Answers may include:

Deuteronomy 7:9: God is faithful.

Deuteronomy 32:4: God is faithful, without iniquity, just, and upright.

Psalm 147:5: God is great, abundant in power, and His understanding is beyond measure.

Romans 11:33: God is wise and unsearchable.

1 Corinthians 14:33: God is peaceful.

Page 68

Page 91

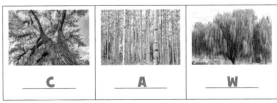

C   A   W

Page 93

B	E	A	V	E	R	Q	W	W	X	Z
P	M	N	V	B	E	M	I	C	E	K
V	X	K	M	Y	Z	S	L	D	F	J
R	A	S	P	E	N	E	L	I	B	E
L	S	V	Q	N	W	P	O	J	K	L
C	O	Y	O	T	E	L	W	M	P	K

Page 118

1. **does not have**

2. **four**

3. **30–60**

Page 120

R	A	C	C	O	O	N	Z	Q	P	M
W	C	X	J	K	K	D	B	E	A	R
L	J	K	N	T	R	E	W	D	H	L
S	Q	U	I	R	R	E	L	F	O	X
Q	K	V	Y	K	W	R	O	J	K	Q
S	O	R	O	P	O	S	S	U	M	P

Page 126

Shorter days cause a change in the amount of light, and the trees begin preparing for the winter.

Page 128

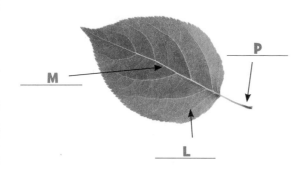

M

P

L

Page 130

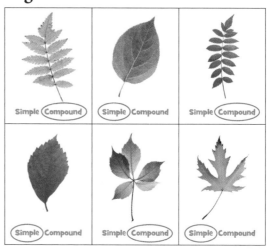

Simple (Compound) | (Simple) Compound | Simple (Compound)

(Simple) Compound | Simple (Compound) | (Simple) Compound

Page 146

1. **above**

2. **slowly**

3. **shade**

Page 150

Approximately 28

Page 156

Canopy

Understory

Forest

Floor

Page 158

B	L	O	O	D	R	O	O	T	P	M
W	C	X	J	K	K	D	B	U	A	R
L	J	K	N	T	R	E	W	L	H	L
S	Q	U	T	R	I	L	L	I	U	M
Q	K	V	Y	K	W	R	O	P	K	Q
D	A	F	F	O	D	I	L	S	M	P

Page 169

P	F	Z	Y	E	A	S	T	X	P	H
M	U	S	H	R	O	O	M	U	K	Y
K	N	F	J	L	M	N	W	Q	Z	P
X	G	K	L	Q	S	B	N	M	L	H
F	U	N	G	I	W	R	Z	P	K	A
J	S	K	Q	O	E	N	Z	Y	M	E

Page 210

Z	X	C	V	P	I	R	A	N	H	A
M	O	W	J	A	C	U	N	D	A	B
E	S	O	R	Q	P	R	T	S	L	F
Q	C	A	P	A	R	I	E	R	K	X
C	A	P	I	N	E	C	O	N	E	R
A	R	A	P	A	I	M	A	I	B	I

Page 182

1. keystone

2. food

3. pollution

Page 190

Parasite – An organism that lives inside or on a different organism and receives nutrients from it.

Commensalism – A type of relationship in which two organisms have a relationship, but only one receives a benefit.

Parasitism – A relationship when a parasite lives on a host.

Page 204

1. **southern**

2. **do**

3. **warm and rainy**

4. **smallest**

Page 220

Page 226

1. 100

2. upper

3. darker

4. evaporating

5. dense

Page 258

1. mammals

2. bigger

3. canopy

4. prehensile

Page 264

1. **large**

2. **very little**

3. **need**

4. **trees**

Page 290

1. continent

2. savannahs

3. Africa

4. wet

Page 292

To adjust or change for certain conditions or a particular environment.

Page 300

Answers may include:

Deep roots reach water that is deep.

The tangled roots hold the soil together tightly. Water tends to get trapped in the tight soil around the tangled roots. This keeps water available for the grass longer.

Page 306

1. There usually isn't enough water to support many trees.

2. Fire

Page 320

1. keystone

2. tusks

3. herd

They use their tusks like a shovel to dig holes in the ground. If the elephant reaches stored water, the holes fill up with that water to create a small watering hole.

Page 326

Z	X	Y	T	U	K	L	M	D	N	G
E	L	E	P	H	A	N	T	R	B	I
B	M	E	E	R	K	A	T	A	V	R
R	C	A	P	A	R	I	E	P	C	A
A	N	T	E	L	O	P	E	O	X	F
Y	K	J	H	G	F	D	S	E	Z	F
J	P	K	Q	G	A	Z	E	L	L	E

Page 330

Answers may include:

Zebras smell predators and when alerting the other zebras, they are also alerting the ostriches. An ostrich has good vision and while alerting the other ostriches, they are also alerting the zebras.

Page 346

Answers may include:

God only created humans in His image.

Page 354

Steward means to manage.